BEYOND INEQUALITIES 2005

Women
in South Africa

SRDC
Southern African Research
and Documentation Centre

CALS
Centre for Applied
Legal Studies

UNIVERSITY *of the*
WESTERN CAPE

UNIVERSITY OF WESTERN CAPE
GENDER EQUITY UNIT
Private Bag X17, Bellville 7535, Cape Town, South Africa
Tel 27 21 696 5982 Fax 27 21 959 1314
Email gender@uwc.ac.za

UNIVERSITY OF THE WITWATERSRAND
GENDER RESEARCH PROGRAMME
CENTRE FOR APPLIED LEGAL STUDIES
Private Bag 3, Wits University 2050, South Africa
Tel 27 11 717 8600 Fax 27 11 403 2341
Email albertync@law.wits.ac.za

SOUTHERN AFRICAN RESEARCH AND DOCUMENTATION CENTRE (SARDC)
Women In Development Southern Africa Awareness (WIDSAA) Programme
P.O. Box 5690, Harare, Zimbabwe
Tel 263 4 791141/3   Fax 263 4 791271
Email widsaa@sardc.net   sardc@sardc.net   sardc@maputo.sardc.net
Website http://www.sardc.net

ISBN 1-77910-027-2

Citation: University of Western Cape Gender Equity Unit, University of Witswatersrand
Centre for Applied Legal Studies and SARDC WIDSAA, *Beyond Inequalities* 2005: *Women in
South Africa*, Cape Town, Johannesburg and Harare, 2006.

Available in Book form in English and at the Virtual Library for Southern Africa www.sardc.net

Cover Design	Paul Wade and Tonely Ngwenya
Text Design	Tonely Ngwenya
Layout/DTP	Tonely Ngwenya, Arnoldina Chironda
Production Coordination	Eunice Kadiki
Origination/Print	DS Print Media, Johannesburg

BEYOND INEQUALITIES

2005

Women
in South Africa

A profile of Women in South Africa
produced by the
University of Western Cape Gender Equity Unit,
University of the Witswatersrand Centre for Applied Legal Studies,
and the
Women in Development Southern Africa Awareness (WIDSAA) Programme
of the
Southern African Research and Documentation Centre (SARDC)

Written by
Mary Hames, Karin Koen and Patricia Handley of Gender Equity Unit
and Professor Cathi Albertyn of the Centre for Applied Legal Studies

WIDSAA is a southern African partnership initiative with national partners in member countries of the Southern African Development Community (SADC). Production of this profile was funded by the Southern Africa Regional Office of the Humanist Institute for Co-operation with Developing Countries (HIVOS).

Women in Development Southern Africa Awareness (WIDSAA)
a programme of the
Southern African Research and Documentation Centre (SARDC)

WIDSAA Programme Staff
Barbara Lopi, Head of Programme
Priscilla Mng'anya, Senior Researcher/Writer
Petronella Mugoni, Programme Assistant/Researcher
Washington Midzi, Research Assistant
Chenai Mufanawejingo, Documentalist
Tendai Gandanzara, Project Accountant

WIDSAA Reviewers
Barbara Lopi
Patience Zirima
Nakatiwa Mulikita
Saeanna Chingamuka

External Reviewer
Susan Nkomo

Series Editor
Alice Kwaramba

Gender Reference Group
Elsie Alexander, Sociology Lecturer Botswana
Bookie M Kethusegile-Juru, Assistant Secretary General, SADC Parliamentary
Forum, Namibia
Susan Nkomo, Chief Executive Officer in the Office on the Status of Women,
    South Africa
Nomboniso Gasa, Researcher/Consultant, South Africa
Thembayena Dlamini, Consultant/Gender Specialist, Swaziland
Terezinah da Silva, Gender Consultant and Chairperson of Forum Mulher,
    Mozambique
Prof. Ruth Meena, Gender Consultant, Tanzania
Pamela Mhlanga, Director of Programmes, SARDC Mozambique
Barbara Lopi, WIDSAA Head of Programme

PREFACE

*B*eyond Inequalities, a series of publications profiling the status of
women in southern Africa, has played a significant role in contributing to knowledge on the role of men and women in development in the region, and the efforts being made at mainstreaming
gender-equality concerns at all levels. The first set of profiles, present-
ing the situation of men and women in 12 SADC countries, were published between 1998 and 2000. This new *Beyond Inequalities* series is an
update on the status of women, in the context of the dynamic changes,
new challenges, setbacks and opportunities that have occurred in the
last few years, particularly since publication of the first series.

The analysis of the status of women in SADC is located within some
important frameworks, chief amongst them being the Beijing
Declaration and Platform for Action (BDPFA), resulting from the
United Nations Fourth World Conference on Women held in Beijing,
China, and the 1997 SADC Declaration on Gender and Development,
including the 1998 Addendum on the Prevention and Eradication of
Violence Against Women and Children. The region has experienced
rapid socio-economic and political shifts, and the focus is increasingly
geared towards ensuring that the region accelerates efforts towards
economic emancipation. Thus, key developments such as the New
Partnership for Africa's Development (NEPAD), and the Millennium
Development Goals (MDGs) in particular, identify new benchmarks
and targets for governments to achieve in order to realise human
development and, by extension, equality of opportunities and outcomes for all.

This is a significant time in southern Africa and beyond, in that it is the
eve of the end of the decade for achieving women's full equality in line
with the BDPFA. The milestones can be identified in the region's response
to the challenges of policy, institutional and legislative developments.
Twelve SADC member states now have gender/women's empowerment
policies in place; Swaziland and Mozambique's policy development
processes are at an advanced stage. All countries identified critical areas
of concern from the BDPFA, and it is significant that a majority identified
issues of women's health (later including HIV and AIDS), economic
empowerment and education as key areas for targeted action. In the political arena, there is a slow but upward trend of women occupying seats of
power in SADC, particularly in politics, where representation in the legislatures rose from an average of 17 percent to almost 20 percent in the last
five years and continues to rise toward SADC's 30 percent target, which
has been surpassed in some countries, notably South Africa where 43 percent of the cabinet are women.

There have been advances in legislation, particularly on issues of
sexual and domestic violence, with some countries widening the definition of rape to include marital rape, and tightening remedies for survivors of domestic violence to include removal of the abuser from the
home. All SADC countries have now ratified the Convention on the
Elimination of All Forms of Discrimination Against Women (CEDAW),
and all have adopted, but few have ratified, the Protocol to the African
Charter on Human and Peoples' Rights on the Rights of Women in
Africa.

University of Western Cape Gender Equity Unit

The Gender Equity Unit (GEU) has been based at the University of the Western Cape (UWC) since its establishment in 1993. Its goals are to develop a statistical profile of the gender composition of the workplace at UWC; analyse the position of women on campus in all aspects of university life, including decision-making structures, appointments, promotions, research and teaching; study the achievements and access of female students to university programmes and develop a curriculum on women and gender for the under-, and postgraduate levels. The GEU runs mentoring programmes such as the writing and publishing programme for women.

University of the Witwatersrand Centre for Applied Legal Studies

The Gender Research Project (GRP) of the Centre for Applied Legal Studies was formed in 1992 within University of the Witwatersrand. The GRP seeks to promote gender equality and social justice for women and men, with a particular focus on disadvantaged women. The project specializes in legal and socio-legal research in a number of areas of law and human rights, including constitutional issues, customary law, reproductive rights, employment, and family law, access to justice, violence against women, HIV and AIDS, policy processes and the political participation of women. The GRP produces quality research, which enables South Africans to participate effectively in policy-making and law reform, as well as the development of the legal and constitutional frameworks to shape these processes and their products.

Institutional structures such as gender/women's ministries, departments, units, and gender desks, were put in place or their mandates expanded to take on the challenge of implementing the ambitious plans to achieve full equality between men and women, and in particular women's empowerment. The SADC Gender Unit, by virtue of the restructuring exercise of the institution, has also been integrated into the Department of Strategic Planning, Gender and Policy Harmonisation to ensure it continues to play a pivotal role in facilitating gender mainstreaming. Most of these structures, however, are inadequately resourced and skilled, and thus remain relatively weak and unable to implement gender policies and plans adequately; this has largely limited the effectiveness of post-Beijing plans and initiatives. Gender and/or women's empowerment groups continue to play a role in bridging this implementation divide, and are influential in the policy and programmatic arenas, although they face their own challenges.

Whilst milestones have been achieved, there have been setbacks, and new issues have emerged. Some of the greatest threats to human, and in particular women's development, are HIV and AIDS and other communicable diseases such as malaria and tuberculosis. There are an estimated 14 million HIV-infected people in the SADC region, representing approximately 37 percent of the global total; women and girls being the hardest hit as both the infected and affected. The pandemic has placed a heavy toll on women's labour through increased unpaid care work, as well as further compromising their sexuality rights by virtue of the imbalance of power intersecting with negative cultural beliefs and practices socially and in intimate relationships. The current *Beyond Inequalities* series seeks to highlight some of these issues, and women's coping mechanisms, as well as government and other stakeholder responses.

Although there is now an acknowledgment that HIV and AIDS are development challenges, their gender dimension and links to human rights remain a challenge. The SADC Declaration on HIV and AIDS adopted in July 2003, places a premium on increasing access to treatment and awareness, and, to some extent recognises gender as a key variable. Resource allocation to address the multi-dimensional nature of the pandemic remains weak in most countries and very few countries in SADC are close to reaching the target of universal access to treatment, though some have targeted programmes for pregnant women to prevent parent-to-child transmission.

Poverty remains high, with 40 percent of the population in SADC living in extreme poverty. The SADC Executive Secretary recently observed that poverty reduction strategies employed by governments in the region are trailing behind in terms of meeting the benchmarks set by the MDGs, to halve poverty by 2015. In fact, SADC economies have generally experienced slow growth in recent years, with few exceptions. The average growth rate of 3.23 percent in 2002 falls below half of the seven percent target growth rate set in the MDGs, if poverty and other development indicators are to be effectively addressed in the next few years. A compromised economic outlook and high poverty hits the most vulnerable hardest, in this case women and children, with a corresponding negative impact on their ability to meet their most basic needs. Ten years after the Beijing Conference, poverty remains one of the biggest challenges in the region.

The *Beyond Inequalities* series has been updated based on the conviction (highlighted in the last series) that information is a strategic resource for socio-economic development. Information can catalyse development, and unless the players have access to reliable information on the complexities and nature of gender relations and how they intersect with development, effective response and the process of positive change will remain slow, and ineffective. The profiles thus identify issues, challenges, limitations and opportunities for accelerating the pace to achieve gender-equality in SADC, through identifying the roles of men and women, their relationships to economic, political and social resources to achieve the highest level of human development.

The series, including this update, was conceptualised and has been implemented by SARDC WIDSAA, in collaboration with partners at national level. WIDSAA aims to contribute to the improvement of the status of women in the SADC region, through awareness-building and collecting, documenting and disseminating relevant, timely, quality and current information to a range of strategic stakeholders. In particular, the information is targeted to policy makers, researchers, media, co-operating partners, development agencies, and the non-governmental sector.

To update this set of *Beyond Inequalities* profiles, a concept paper was developed and shared with partners in SADC countries for comments and critique. The concept paper outlined the rationale and methodology for approaching the updating exercise. This was followed by terms of reference for partner organisations to co-ordinate the research and writing of the profiles, which also included guidelines on style and presentation of the drafts by the researchers.

Each partner organisation identified a multi-disciplinary team of researchers to conduct the work on the profiles. This was coupled with a survey of the previous *Beyond Inequalities* series to determine the nature and extent of access and utilisation, in order to enrich the updating exercise and provide pointers towards a more effective dissemination strategy. The drafts were reviewed by individuals and at annual partners meetings where the researchers presented their initial or working drafts to a group of 25-30 people for critique. This was preceded by a Gender Reference Group meeting to review the drafts and provide guidance on content, methodology and management of the updating exercise.

The partner organisations and researchers held validation workshops with national stakeholders, and some constituted working committees that provided input at various stages of development of the drafts. The methodology for production of the profiles was thus a participatory one, to ensure wide ownership and participation in the process of development and production.

The profiles are all similarly presented in four parts. Part I gives a situational analysis, Part II provides information on achievements and constraints in the context of policies and programmes, and Part III discusses the way forward. Part IV contains references and a bibliography of materials used. Annexes follow at the end of the publication.

Many challenges lie ahead. Ten years of working on achieving gender-equality after Beijing has produced mixed results, with a rollback of some gains made. This *Beyond Inequalities* series gives current insights and perspectives on achievements, gaps and the way forward, as well as areas where opportunities can be found for revitalising processes or finding new direction. The focus of the next decade is on delivery of policies and programmes, and the *Beyond Inequalities* series provides information on what has worked and what has not, and what can be strengthened or abandoned as gender activists in SADC shape an agenda for the future.

SARDC

The Southern African Research and Documentation Centre (SARDC) is an independent regional information resource centre, which seeks to enhance the effectiveness of key development processes in the SADC region through the collection, production and dissemination of information, and enabling the capacity to generate and use information. SARDC has five main areas of focus, which are pursued by separate specialist departments for environment and water resources, gender, democracy and governance, regional economic development, and human development. SARDC has offices in Harare and Maputo and partners in all SADC member states. Founding Patron was the late *Mwalimu* Julius Nyerere.

WIDSAA

Women In Development Southern Africa Awareness (WIDSAA) is the gender programme of SARDC. The programme was established in 1994 to serve as a catalyst and information service to the SADC region's governments, parliaments, NGOs and agencies, the media and the public in the formulation of policy affecting women. WIDSAA's objective is for SADC women to be empowered and advanced, and structures engendered to realise equality and equity.

HIVOS

The Humanist Institute for Co-operation with Developing Countries (HIVOS) is a Dutch non-governmental organisation, which operates on the basis of humanistic values. HIVOS aims to contribute towards a free, just, and sustainable world. The organisation is committed to the poor and marginalised and to organisations with similar interests in countries in the South, including Africa, central Asia and southeast Europe. Sustainable improvement of their situation is the ultimate benchmark for HIVOS' work. An important cornerstone is strengthening of the position of women in society.

National Policy for Women's Empowerment and Gender Equality, 2000   Box 1

Principles

South Africa's definition and goals towards achieving gender equality are guided by a vision of human rights, which incorporates acceptance of equal inalienable rights of women and men. This idea is a fundamental tenet under the Bill of Rights of The Constitution of the Republic of South Africa, 1996 (Act 108 of 1996). It emerged from a long period of struggle for a democratic society that respects and promotes the rights of all its citizens irrespective of race, gender, class, age, disability, etc. (Bill of Rights, Section 9.1 to 9.4).

Goals

- To ensure that there is equality of all persons by eliminating sexism and racism in the Constitution of South Africa. Women's rights must be seen as human rights.
- To ensure that customary, cultural and religious practices are subjected to equality by changing policies that have hindered women's access to basic needs, the economy and decision-making.
- To ensure that appropriate training to improve knowledge, skills and attitudes in gender analysis and gender equality is provided to all policy-makers and strategic and operational managers.

Focus

- Development of a National Policy Framework by reviewing existing policies and institutionalising women's empowerment and gender equality in line department.
- Development of a Gender Mainstreaming Strategy.
- Adoption of a National Policy Framework and receipt of ministerial commitment.
- Development of Provincial Gender Action Plans and Gender Mainstreaming Strategies.

Priority areas

- Violence;
- Poverty;
- Health;
- Education;
- Economic empowerment;
- Institutional mechanisms; and
- Decision-making.

Implementation

Co-ordinating body: Office on The Status of Women

Other stakeholders

Government ministries and agencies, including NGOs, CBOs, private sector and donor communities.

SOURCE Extracts from South Africa's National Policy Framework for Women's Empowerment and Gender Equality, OSW, 2000 and South Africa's first progress report on the Beijing Platform for Action, 2002.

CONTENTS

List of Tables, Figures and Boxes

ACKNOWLEDGEMENTS

S ARDC WIDSAA would like to thank all of our national partners and members of the Gender Reference Group (GRG) for their active participation in a continuing process to provide accessible and current information on gender equality, and the challenges and opportunities in realising women's empowerment in southern Africa. We also want to thank readers and reviewers at national and regional levels, who gave constructive comments on the content and production of the profile. In all, approximately 25 researchers participated in the production of the updated profiles for Botswana, Malawi, Mozambique, Namibia, South Africa, Zambia and Zimbabwe. More than 30 people reviewed the drafts.

We are grateful to the Humanist Institute for Co-operation with Developing Countries (HIVOS) for its financial contribution towards this project's realisation. Particular recognition goes to Corina Straatsma, the Director of the Southern Africa Regional Office of HIVOS for accepting to fund the proposal to produce national gender profiles under the *Beyond Inequalities* series. Special thanks go to the SARDC Executive Director, Phyllis Johnson, and the Deputy Director, Munetsi Madakufamba, who supported the process throughout. To our colleagues in other SARDC departments, Tafadzwa Ndoro, Charles Hakata, Chipo Muvezwa, Dambudzo Jambwa, Clever Mafuta, Suzanna Gemo and their staff who assisted in so many ways, we are grateful that you contributed to ensure that the job undertaken to produce this profile was well done.

Most of all, recognition goes to our partner organisation in South Africa, the Gender Equity Unit of the University of Western Cape and Professor Cathi Albertyn of the Centre for Applied Legal Studies at the University of the Witwatersrand. Without them, this enormous task would not have been accomplished. All those who have not been named, but were involved with the process in a way, at any time, are gratefully acknowledged.

SARDC WIDSAA Team, Harare

The Gender Equity Unit would like to thank SARDC WIDSAA for affording us the opportunity to be part of this important and exciting venture. Appreciation goes to the Gender Reference Group for the valuable input and comments. We are heavily indebted to Professor Cathi Albertyn of the Centre for Applied Legal Studies at the University of the Witwatersrand for her contribution, and to Susan Nkomo, the Chief Executive Officer in the Office on the Status of Women, in the Office of the President in South Africa, for extensively reviewing the document and providing needed information where there were gaps.

We are also acknowledging the following people for their critical insight and contributions: Dr Cheryl Hendricks, Dr Desiree Lewis, Dr Yvette Abrahams, Professor Amanda Gouws, Penny Paranzee and Glenise Levendal.

The Women's Net is greatly acknowledged for their informational contribution by making Dr Neva Seidman Makgetla's research on *Women and the Economy in South Africa*, available and accessible during the research for this publication.

A thousand thanks to Nontle Beja and Vanessa Ludwig for their patience and endless political debates regarding women and gender in the office.

Finally, recognition and thanks to the University of the Western Cape, which is consistent in believing that another world is possible.

Mary Hames, Gender Equity Unit Director, University of Western Cape

ACRONYMS

ABET	Adult Basic Education Trust
ACDP	African Christian Democratic Party
AGOA	African Growth and Opportunities Act
AIDS	Acquired Immune Deficiency Syndrome
ANC	African National Congress
ARV	Anti Retro-Viral
AU	African Union
BPFA	Beijing Platform For Action
BEE	Black Economic Empowerment
CBO	Community-Based Organisation
CEDAW	Convention on the Elimination of all forms of Discrimination Against Women
CGE	Commission on Gender Equality
COSATU	Congress of South African Trade Unions
CSS	Central Statistical Service
DA	Democratic Alliance
DLA	Department of Land Affairs
DSD	Department of Social Development
DTI	Department of Trade and Industry
DVA	Domestic Violence Act
FF	Freedom Front
FGM	Female Genital Mutilation
GAP	Gender Advocacy Programme
GDP	Gross Domestic Product
GEAR	Growth Employment and Redistribution
GEMSA	Gender and Media Southern Africa
GETT	Gender and Education Task Team
GEU	Gender Equity Unit
GFP	Gender Focal Points
GRG	Gender Reference Group
HDI	Human Development Index
HIV	Human Immunodeficiency Virus
HIVOS	Humanist Institute for Co-operation with Developing Countries
HRDS	Human Resources Development Strategy
HSRC	Human Sciences Research Council
IBA	Independent Broadcasting Authority
ICASA	Independent Communications Authority of South Africa
ICT	Information Communication Technology
IFP	Inkhata Freedom Party
ILO	International Labour Organisation
ISSA	Institute for Satellite Software Applications
KZN	KwaZulu Natal
MDG	Millennium Development Goals
MISA	Media Institute of Southern Africa
MRC	Medical Research Council
NCCEMD	National Committee for Confidential Enquiries into Maternal Deaths
NEPAD	New Partnership for Africa's Development

NGO	Non Governmental Organisation
NICRO	National Institute of Crime and Rehabilitation of Offenders
NP/NNP	New National Party
NSDS	National Skills Development Strategy
OSW	Office on the Status of Women
PAC	Pan Africanist Congress
PEP	Post Exposure Prophylaxis
PMTCT	Prevention of Mother-to-Child Transmission
POWA	People Opposed to Women's Abuse
RDP	Reconstruction and Development Programme
RNCS	Revised National Curriculum Statement
SABC	South African Broadcasting Corporation
SADC	Southern African Development Community
SADHS	South African Demographic and Health Survey
SALGA	South African Local Government Association
SANEF	South African National Editors' Forum
SANGOCO	South African Non-Government Congress
SAPS	South African Police Service
SARDC	Southern African Research and Documentation Centre
SAWIMA	South African Women in Mining Association
SAWEN	South African Women Entrepreneurs' Network
SDI	Special Development Initiatives
SMME	Small, Micro and Medium Enterprises
STD	Sexually Transmitted Disease
STI	Sexually Transmitted Infection
SWEAT	Sex Workers' Education and Training
TAC	Treatment Action Campaign
TWIB	Technology for Women in Business
UCDP	United Christian Democratic Party
UDP	United Democratic Party
UIF	Unemployment Insurance Fund
UWC	University of the Western Cape
VCT	Voluntary Counselling and Testing
WEPU	Women's Empowerment Unit
WIDSAA	Women in Development Southern Africa Awareness
WNC	Women's National Coalition
WOESA	Women in Oil and Energy in South Africa

SOUTH AFRICA DEVELOPMENT INDICATORS

Official Name	Republic of South Africa
Capital City	Cape Town (Legislative) and Pretoria (Executive)
Freedom Day	27 April 1994
Head of State	President Thabo Mbeki
Last Election	April 2004
Ruling Party	African National Congress
Legislature	Parliament
Languages	English, Afrikaans, IsiNdebele, Sesotho, Sepedi, SiSwati, Xitsonga, Setswana, Tshivenda, IsiXhosa and IsiZulu
Land Area	1,219,090 sq km

POPULATION

Total (2005 mid-year estimates)	46.9 million
	women 51.2 %
	men 48.8 %
Population Growth Rate	0.92 %

HEALTH

Life Expectancy at Birth	47.1 years
Birth Rate	23.8/1,000 population
Death Rate	18.42 /1,000 population
Total Fertility Rate	2.8
Infant Mortality Rate	53.6/1,000 live births
Maternal Mortality Rate	230/100,000

EDUCATION

Adult Literacy Rate	85.9 %
	women 85.7 %
	men 87 %

ECONOMY

Gross Domestic Product	US$213.1 billion
Gross Domestic Product (per capita)	US$4,574
Gross Domestic Product (composition by sector 2001)	
Agriculture	4.4 %
Industry	28.9 %
Services	66.7 %
Export	US$56.50 billion (2004)
Import	US$57.600 billion (2004)
Currency South African Rand (100 cents)	ZAR6.8701=US$1 (August, 2006)

Note All statistics are for 2003 unless otherwise specified.

SOURCES
Statistics South Africa, Labour Force Survey, 2001
Statistics South Africa, Census in Brief 2001, Second Edition. Pretoria, 2003
http://www.sadc.int
http://www.statssa.gov.za
http://www.reservebank.co.za

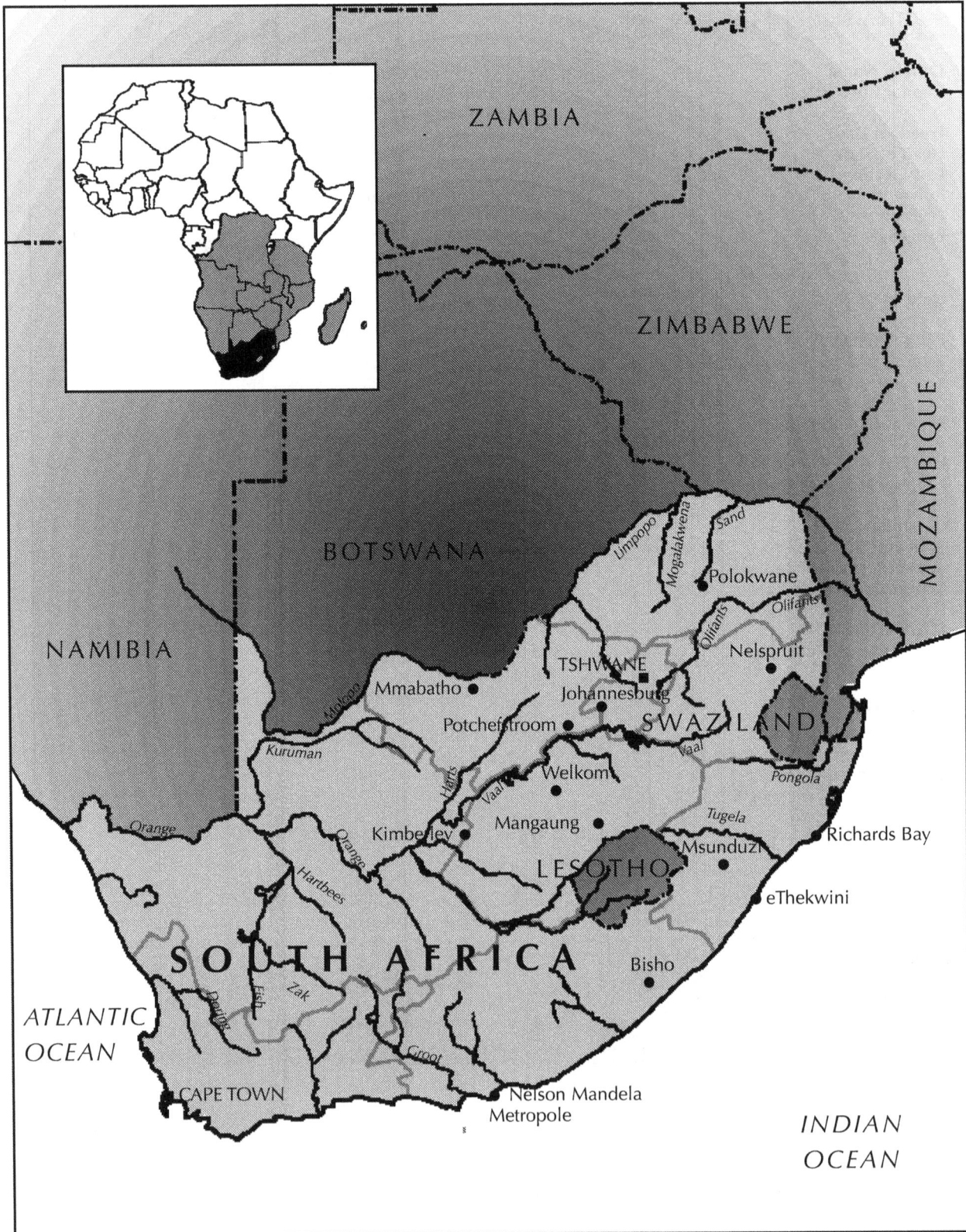

ZAMBIA

ZIMBABWE

MOZAMBIQUE

BOTSWANA

Limpopo

Mogalakwena

Sand

Polokwane

Olifants

Olifants

NAMIBIA

TSHWANE

Nelspruit

Mmabatho

Johannesburg

Molopo

Potchefstroom

SWAZILAND

Kuruman

Vaal

Harts

Welkom

Pongola

Vaal

Orange

Tugela

Mangaung

Kimberley

Richards Bay

Orange

Msunduzi

Hartbees

LESOTHO

eThekwini

SOUTH AFRICA

Zak

Bisho

Fish

ATLANTIC
OCEAN

Doring

Groot

CAPE TOWN

Nelson Mandela
Metropole

INDIAN
OCEAN

INTRODUCTION

This national gender profile describes South Africa's progress and challenges in achieving women's empowerment and gender equality goals. It measures the South African government's achievements against its stated commitments both within its supreme legislation – the Constitution, its policies, the legislative framework it has put in place, as well as the international agreements it is party to. The publication also assesses the impact of the institutional mechanisms for women's advancement that South Africa has put in place since 1994.

The approach in gathering information has been comprehensive. The review is based on statistical data taken from the National Statistical Services to indicate major social trends. It also draws from government departments' reports of programmes implemented since 1994, the outcome of provincial and national "Conversations among Women", which took place between July and August 2003; and the Office on the Status of Women (OSW) Audits (1998, 2002, and 2003) of systems in place to enable gender mainstreaming. Information from South Africa's reports on the implementation of the Beijing Platform For Action (BPFA) as well as the SADC Declaration on Gender and Development was used in compiling this national gender profile.

The 1994 elections in South Africa brought significant changes in the social, political and economic environment, with two subsequent elections in 1999 and 2004 consolidating these changes. The anticipated impact of these changes on women was comprehensively examined in *Beyond Inequalities: Women in South Africa*, published three years after the first democratic election. This publication thus assesses the progress made in South Africa's journey to eradicate inequalities and the progress towards gender equality from 1997 when the last gender profile was published.

Objectives

The purpose of this national profile is to update the situation of women in South Africa since the first profile was compiled in 1997. It highlights what developments have taken place in gender and development since then and the challenges the country still faces in this regard. The specific objective is to present the situation of women in South Africa and analyse policies, programmes and mechanisms that have been put in place towards ending gender inequalities, and that contribute to gender transformation and women's empowerment in the country.

Significance of the profile

This profile is important because it brings to the attention of the policymakers pertinent issues that still need urgent attention in order to address glaring problems faced by women in South Africa, including issues such as poverty, illiteracy, gender-based violence, inequality, oppression, and HIV and AIDS. It is also the only document of its kind, which provides relevant qualitative and quantitative data on a wide range of topics pertaining to women in one report; and it clearly presents gaps in (qualitative and quantitative terms) on issues, which reflect the situation of women in South Africa today.

Methodology
The profile presents qualitative information on women and men in South Africa and, where necessary, quantitative data was used to complement and provide a more comprehensive picture of the South African society.

Theoretical perspective
The guiding analytical framework in this profile was informed by the intersection between women in development and gender perspectives. Using this perspective the analysis on the position of women in South Africa in relation to that of men is presented including the different roles played by women and men as well as ideologies shaping their lives. The analysis was also conducted from a development perspective, and other development processes that have taken place in South Africa and how these have impacted on the role and status of women in particular. By using this analytical framework certain themes and topical areas/issues key in shaping women's empowerment agenda in South Africa are identified.

Outline of the profile
Part I presents a broad situation analysis of the status of women and their roles in some key areas. These include women and the economy (both macro and micro economic), representation in politics and private sector, access to education and technology, health services and living environment, media, culture and religion, poverty and violence against women. It also highlights some key gender milestones attained in South Africa since independence in 1994.

Part II focuses on policies and programmes addressing gaps and challenges in decision-making, access to health, education, economic resources, land and the media, as well as an assessment of areas where major policies have been effected. It evaluates the gains, obstacles, and challenges for South African women in their struggles for long-term and sustainable gender transformation.

Part III presents the way forward and a brief conclusion of the gains that women have made as well as the challenges that they still face and areas in which policy and programme interventions are required. Emphasis is placed on the concerns outlined in the Beijing Platform For Action, SADC Gender and Development Declaration, South Africa's Gender Policy as well as other regional and international gender equality commitments.

Part IV contains a reference of materials used in compiling the profile as well as a bibliography.

PART I
SITUATION ANALYSIS

Background and national context
In 2006, South Africa celebrates the Fiftieth anniversary of the 1956 Women's March to the Union Building. That historic march on 9 August has resulted in the day, 9 August, being declared a women's day in the country since the establishment of the first democratic government in 1994.

Since attaining democracy, South Africa has made substantial achievements in women empowerment and the advancement towards gender equality. The year 2006 also marks the tenth year of the South African Constitution, which has non-racism and non-sexism as its core values.

However, some challenges remain. South Africa's definition of, and goals towards, achieving women empowerment and gender equality are guided by a vision of human rights which incorporates acceptance of equal and inalienable rights of all men and women. This ideal is a fundamental tenet under the Bill of Rights of the Constitution of the Republic of South Africa, 1996 (Act 108 of 1996).

The South African Constitution creates an enabling environment for effective gender mainstreaming. In line with the South African Constitution, South Africa's National Policy Framework for Women Empowerment and Gender Equality is based on a vision of a society in which women and men are able to realise their full potential and to participate as equal partners in creating a just and prosperous society for all.

This updated national gender profile gives some insight into the achievements as well as gaps in South Africa's advancement as a democracy driven by a human rights approach to development. In this way, the profile informs on both the achievements as well as further steps to be taken.

The South African approach to achieving gender equality draws on the strategy of gender mainstreaming. This strategy emphasises the responsibility of all government structures, agencies and civil society, in directing the development agenda within governance in a way that ensures the realisation of gender equality. The first democratic government addressed many aspects of women's political participation and social citizenship.

The early legislative gains included issues pertaining to personal autonomy, reproductive choice and gender-based violence. In addition, institutional mechanisms were put in place to ensure the promotion and the protection of gender equality including the establishment of the Commission on Gender Equality, the formalisation of a Joint Monitoring Committee on the Improvement of the Quality of Life and Status of Women as well as the Office on the Status of Women within the Presidency.

While the extensive legislative framework was in place by the second democratic election (1999), intractable problems of transformation surfaced. The socio-economic indicators of inequality suggest that the new policies and the enabling legislative framework have not substantially impacted on women's lives on the ground. The challenges experienced in implementing the new laws exposed the widening gap between legislative and policy frameworks, and the realities on the ground.

By the end of the first decade of freedom, as the first national report to the United Nations on the implementation of the Beijing Platform of Action observed, despite the abolition of legislative discrimination, the legacy of structured and entrenched inequalities which characterised apartheid were still manifested in the lives of the majority of South Africans. The picture of poverty amidst plenty remained as well as the socio-economic marginalisation of women. The Beijing+5 report also pointed out that the challenge for the next five years of democracy i.e. 2000-2005 was that of implementation.

As President Mbeki was to point out in the State of the Nation Address in 2003, "… we must also refer to the important matter of gender equality. Some progress is being made in government to address this issue. And in the private sector and civil society, the campaign on the rights of women has started at least to form part of the national discourse. But society still lags in terms of actual implementation, particularly in mainstreaming gender issues on development and poverty eradication. Within government, we will continue to insist on the implementation of the National Framework for Women's Empowerment and Gender Equality. Concretely, we will soon introduce a system through which gender representation targets and content of programmes become part of the core performance criteria of every government institution and manager."[1]

Thus, by 2003 emphasis had shifted from the creation of the enabling environment through the creation of legal and policy measures, to that of elaborating appropriate implementation mechanisms for gender mainstreaming. Within this context, it was necessary to clarify the specific

and different roles of stakeholders within the National Gender Machinery as well as those of all state institutions and civil society organisations.

Gender milestones
Since 1997, when the last *Beyond Inequalities: Women in South Africa* was published, numerous policies and programmes for women, as well as impressive figures of women, especially in politics and decision-making positions, have been recorded. For instance, in quantitative terms, women's participation in public life since 1998 has been encouraging.

The increase of women in parliament from 27 percent in 1994, 30 percent in 1999 to 32.75 percent in 2005 contributed significantly in putting women's issues on the national agenda. South Africa ranks number eight in the world in terms of gender equality in government. The country leapt quickly from a position of 141 in the world before the 1994 elections to number eight, when the African National Congress (ANC) adopted a 30 percent quota on its party list.

Different government departments have adopted a gender perspective in projects such as housing, water, justice, local government, trade and industry and many of the government departments established gender focal points or gender desks, even before the formalisation of the gender machinery in 1997. At the same time, the government has also been reforming and implementing new laws aimed at addressing inequalities and promoting the rights of women.

Regional agreements
South Africa has conformed to the demands of the Southern African Development Community (SADC) Declaration on Gender and Development[2] by meeting the target of 30 percent women represen-

We are proud of the progress although so much still remains to be done – Mbeki Box 2

Writing in the foreword to South Africa's report on the review of progress and implementation of the Beijing Platform for Action, President Thabo Mbeki said: "We are proud of the progress that has been made towards the genuine emancipation and empowerment of the women of South Africa. Nevertheless, we are acutely aware of the fact that so much still remains to be done. …In everything we do, we will continue to be inspired by the vision that our transformation will not be complete until the women of our country are empowered and gender equality in our society has been achieved."

SOURCE Excerpt from *ANC Today*, Volume 5, No. 10, 11-17 March 2005.

tation in political and decision-making positions by 2005. By the second democratic election, South Africa had met the target. The country is moving towards reaching a 50 percent representation of women in political and decision-making positions through the 50/50 campaign. Fifty percent is the target adopted by the African Union and SADC for 2015. The country has also ratified the African Charter on human rights and women's rights.

International instruments
South Africa endorsed and ratified other international multilateral instruments such as the Convention on the Elimination of all forms of Discrimination Against Women (CEDAW), the Beijing Declaration and Platform for Action (BPFA), the Universal Declaration of Human Rights among others, thus committing the country to promoting and protecting people's rights. This has provided the basis for the government to include women in meaningful positions on their party list and subsequently in government structures.

Similarly, these instruments provide the country with a framework for monitoring progress across the critical areas such as poverty, HIV and AIDS, gender-based violence and violence against women, among others, identified by the national, regional and international community as critical to the eradication of entrenched gender inequality.[3]

Millennium Development Goals
The South African Millennium Development Goals report of 2005 indicates that South Africa has already met some of the millennium goals and targets. The report further pointed out that due to its vibrant economic base, "South Africa is well on course to achieve the targets set in the Millennium Declaration."[4] In its efforts to eradicate extreme poverty and hunger, government strategy is aiming at ensuring the following:

- Attending to the basic needs of the poor by providing better infrastructure, such as access to clean water and electricity;
- Giving attention to achieving sustainable developmental goals by creating opportunities for all, for example, giving clinic-based, free primary health care for all, and providing compulsory education for all those aged 7-15 years;
- Providing financial assistance for children, in terms of child grants, and school feeding schemes; and
- Providing comprehensive social security for the vulnerable, for example, people with disabilities and the elderly, by means of social security grants.

According to the report, grants had already benefited over eight million people and they are considered as a safety net against extreme poverty.[5]

POLITICS AND DECISION-MAKING
Political participation of women has increased since 1997. Women have generally become more experienced and entrenched in the political processes. Much of the success can be ascribed to South Africa's commitment to and ratification of various multilateral agreements and conventions in the region as well as internationally. This has provided the basis for the government to include women in meaningful positions on their party list and subsequently in government.

Whilst the involvement of women in political life remains one of the acknowledged dividends of freedom, some have questioned the terms of that participation, and the link between the involvement of women in

South Africa has a woman deputy President   Box 3

South Africa has a woman deputy president, Phumzile Mlambo-Ngcuka. Mlambo-Ngcuka, who is well known in the SADC region for the way that she has used her space in previous ministerial posts to raise gender issues in some of the most resistant quarters, is both a talented woman and a gender activist.

South Africa leads the way in women's participation in cabinet, with 42 percent women ministers, and now a woman deputy president.

President Mbeki has been commended for using the opportunity created by the recent political crisis in South Africa to strengthen women's participation in the executive, and for stating unequivocally that he did so deliberately to make good his and South Africa's commitment to gender equality.

Mbeki's move will strengthen the unstoppable momentum to get our leaders to raise the target for women's representation from 30 to 50 percent at the upcoming SADC summit in Gaborone.

SOURCE Excerpt from Gender and Media Southern Africa (GEMSA) Network's press release, *New SA Deputy President to strengthen 50/50 campaign*, 27 June 2005.

high-level positions in politics and the improvement of the quality of life and status for all women.

In South Africa, as in many countries, there is at present, no women's party contesting at the political level, nor is there a clear articulation of a post-apartheid women's agenda. Therefore, although women form the majority of voters, they have not harnessed that power for specific outcomes. Indeed, it seems there is a long way to go before reference can be made to the existence of a cohesive progressive women's movement in South Africa. However, some steps are being made towards achieving this goal.

Although all the political parties ascribe to the principle of equality as entrenched in the Constitution, it has mainly been the ANC that has systematically used a strict quota system and affirmative action policies for women. The ANC placed women in prime positions on the party list, resulting in the party winning 70 percent of the seats (107 of the 279) that were allocated to women. None of the opposition parties subscribe to a quota system for women.

Women in parliament and cabinet
In spite of the country's progressive stance towards the inclusion of women in parliament, the progress report on the country's implementation of the BPFA indicates that women are unfairly represented in key parliamentary committees. After the first democratic elections in 1994 for instance, women were poorly represented on Committees for Foreign Affairs, Justice, Labour, Mineral and Energy Affairs and Transport. However, women were well represented on the following committees for Arts, Culture and Language, Science and Technology, Health, and

Welfare. All of these portfolios, with the exception of Science and Technology, perhaps, are traditionally regarded as "women's concerns".

As has been noted elsewhere, there has not been a major increase in the representation of women after the 2004 election. This also means that although the intention is to increase women's representation on portfolio committees, it is not possible to do so on a grand scale. The men remain the chairpersons of the "hard" committees while women chair amongst others, the softer committees such as the Joint Monitoring Committee on the Improvement of Quality of Life and Status of Children, Youth and Disabled Persons.

After the June 1999 elections, there was a marked improvement in the new cabinet. Women were well placed in key positions; in charge of Foreign Affairs, Health, the Public Service, Minerals and Energy Affairs, Communication, Housing and Land Affairs. The number of women deputy ministers also increased.

There was also a subsequent increase of women in parliament after the 1999 elections. This was because legislation opened the door to floor crossing in March 2003. Members of opposition parties were afforded the opportunity in the national and provincial legislatures to join the political parties of their choice. The number of women increased to 122 members in the National Assembly. Women from other parties now had a better chance to become Members of Parliament especially when they joined the ANC.

In comparison with the 1999 elections, where women occupied 119 (with the floor crossing the number increased to 122) seats, in 2004 there were 131 women in parliament. The ANC constitutes 82 percent of the total number of women in parliament. There is also an impressive 41.2 percent women ministers and deputy ministers in the country.

Women have moved beyond the critical mass of 30 percent, but have not yet reached 50 percent. There are currently 12 women out of 27 ministers and 10 out of 11 deputy ministers and they fill some of the most crucial positions in Cabinet, namely: Justice, Foreign Affairs, Education, Agriculture and Land, Housing, Home Affairs, Health, Minerals and Energy, Public Service, Water and Forestry, and Communication. The Speaker of Parliament remains a woman.

In 2005, South African President Mbeki made history when he appointed a woman, Phumzile Mlambo-Ngcuka as deputy president.

Representation of women in parliament

Tables 1 and 2 indicate the increase in the representation of women in national and provincial parliaments. The statistics show a slight increase in the number of women in national parliament. If the rate of the increase of between 2.7 and 2.8 percent is something to go by, then parity could only be reached within 30 years or six elections.[6]

Provincial legislatures

Representation at provincial level has shown a slight increase from 24 percent in 1994 to 27.7 percent in 1999, and to 32.3 percent in 2004. The country however still has a challenge to meet the new target of 50 percent female representation.

In the second tier of government, the provincial legislatures, the 2004 elections ensured that 45 percent of the Provincial Premiers are women. There are women Provincial Premiers in the Eastern Cape, Free State, Northern Cape, and the North West Province. The Provincial Premiers have legisla-

tive and executive powers over important matters such as agriculture, casinos, racing, gambling, wagering, cultural affairs, education (except University and Technikon levels), environmental affairs, health services, housing, transport and tourism and trade, amongst others. The Premiers also serve on the President's Co-ordinating Council, which is a consultative forum where the President discusses issues of national, provincial and local governance importance.

The third tier of government represents the local government. Local government is often seen as

Representation of Women in Parliament, 1994 - 2004									Table 1
	1994			**1999**			**2004**		
Party	Total	Women	Women %	Total	Women	Women %	Total	Women	Women %
ANC	252	90	35.7	266	95	35.7	279	104	37
DP/DA	7	1	14	38	6	15.7	50	13	26
IFP	43	10	23	33	9	27.2	28	5	18.5
NP/NNP	82	9	10	28	4	14.2	7	0	0
UDM				14	1	7	9	4	44.4
ACDP	2	0	0	6	2	33	6	2	33
FF				3	0	0	4	0	0
UCDP				3	1	33	3	0	0
PAC	5	1	20	3	0	0	3	0	0
Other				5	2	40	4	0	0
TOTAL	400	111	27.7	400	120	30	400	131	32.75

Source: Compiled based on information obtained from the parliament of South Africa's records for 1994, 1999 and 2004

Women in Provincial Legislatures										Table 2
Provinces	**1994**			**1999**			**2004**			+/-
	Seats	W	%W	Seats	W	%W	Seats	W	%W	
Eastern Cape	56	14	25	63	15	23.8	63	20	31.7	7.9
Gauteng	86	25	29	73	25	34.2	73	31	42.4	8.2
KZN	81	11	13.6	80	21	26.2	80	21	26.2	0
Free State	30	7	23.3	30	7	23.3	30	8	26	-2.7
Limpopo	40	11	27.5	49	15	30.6	49	16	33	2.4
Mpumalanga	30	6	20	30	8	26.6	30	9	30	3.4
Northwest	30	11	37	33	10	30	33	11	33	3
Northern Cape	30	7	24	30	8	26.6	30	11	37	10.4
Western Cape	42	10	23.8	42	10	23.8	42	12	28.5	4.7
TOTAL	425	102	24	430	119	27.7	430	139	32.3	4.6

Source: Compiled based on information obtained from the parliament of South Africa's records for 1994, 1999 and 2004 W = women

the area where democracy and service delivery really matters. Local governments are constitutionally mandated to play key roles in the following areas: housing, electricity, water, garbage collection, recreational and health-care facilities, primary, secondary and adult education programmes, child care facilities, safety and security, roads and infrastructure development. These matters directly affect women's lives.

Local government elections lag behind the national elections but significant policies were implemented since the first local government elections on 1 November 1995 to ensure that women are adequately represented at this level. The 1995 elections reflected the racial profile of the towns. The result was that 40 percent of the local seats were of proportional representation. Whites, mainly in the towns, won 30 percent of the seats, whereas 30 percent of the seats went to Blacks in the townships.

Since the first local government elections, policies and legislation were enacted to deracialise[7] and engender the local government processes. The White Paper on Local Government (1998) and the Municipal Structures Act (1998) are prime examples of the legislative framework that aims at greater representation at the local level.

Although the Municipal Structures Act (1998) enforces a 50 percent representation for ward councillors, it by no means enforces a gender quota because of the absence of a "zebra" proportional representation list. It therefore means that parties are under no obligation to have 50 percent women on their party lists. However, the Act is the closest to any other piece of legislation that promotes women by recommending that every alternate candidate on its list should be a woman.

In spite of the progressive legislation governing local government processes, certain barriers remain intact hindering women's full participation in local governance. Research done by the Gender Advocacy Programme (GAP) in 2002 identified some of the impediments as follows:
- Too many municipalities still rely on written communication, which excludes women who are illiterate or semi-literate;
- Meetings are held at times which are inconvenient for women with childcare and household responsibilities or at venues too far from public transport which many women rely on;
- Depending on public meetings for community participation can limit the participation of women who lack confidence to speak in public or where social norms may dictate that women should not speak in public.

Some researchers have argued that local government could become more effective if the structures and processes integrate gender.[8] This argument supports the fact that if women are part of the planning and implementation processes one is assured that the interest of the whole community has been catered for. It is therefore important that:
- Women must be elected to local government;
- Women must be employed by local government;
- An understanding of women's gender roles and women's inequality must inform all the work of local government; and
- Local government must be accessible to women in civil society.

Since 1994, several NGOs have taken on the role of educating women as active voters, creating access for women to parliament and parliamentary procedures. Political parties have recognised the importance of the "women's vote" and conducted specific campaigns for women voters. The holding of mock parliaments for women and the girl-child are all indicators of the gendered nature of the electoral process.[9]

Electoral and political processes have remained highly patriarchal. The husband, partner or traditional leader continues to play a significant influential role to influence the choices that women take during the electoral processes. It can be argued that although the numbers of women have increased in the decision-making sphere, the woman outside the formal political structures remains at a disadvantage.

ECONOMY

South Africa is classified as a middle-income country, with a population estimated at about 46 million.[10] Since independence, economic growth has been positive, however, the growth has not been strong enough to lower South Africa's high unemployment rate.

Daunting economic problems remain from the apartheid era, especially poverty and lack of economic empowerment among the disadvantaged groups. The 2000 national estimates of poverty and inequality in South Africa indicated that 11 percent of people were living on less than US$1 a day and 34 percent were living on less than US$2 a day.

Women and employment

Women in South Africa as a whole still have lower incomes, higher unemployment, and less access to ownership of assets than men. The racial differences are larger than gender inequalities within racial groups, thus the position of women in the economy, can better be understood if the race issues are also taken into account.

Employment by Race and Gender, 2003[a]						Table 3
	Women			Men		
	Black	Coloured/Asian	White	Black	Coloured/Asian	White
Not economically active	5 567 000	877 000	781 000	3 825 000	506 000	416 000
Employed	3 556 000	840 000	855 000	4 405 000	1 024 000	1 104 000
Unemployed	4 284 000	383 000	92 000	3 200 000	318 000	67 000
Total	13 408 000	2 100 000	1 728 000	11 430 000	848 000	1 588 000
Unemployment rate %	55	31	10	42	24	6
Employment as % of adult population	27	40	49	39	55	70

Source Adapted from September 2003 Labour Force Survey, Statistics South Africa, Pretoria.
Note: a. These data use the expanded definition of unemployment, which includes workers who would take paid work immediately but who are too discouraged to actively seek it.

As Table 3 shows, Black women in South Africa are far less likely to have paid employment than any other group. Women are also more likely to be counted as "economically inactive," that is, to report having neither an earned income of their own nor to be seeking one. Yet, virtually all these women are active in unpaid, mostly reproductive labour, and many receive childcare grants or old-age pensions.

In addition, Black women face far higher rates of unemployment. By 2003, the unemployment rate for Black women was almost 10 times as high as for White men. Black women made up 42 percent of the labour force, but only 30 percent of the employed and 51 percent of the unemployed.

In 2004, data by Statistics South Africa indicated that Black women continue to be the most affected by unemployment, more than seven times than White males.[11] Reasons for high unemployment are attributed to the current economic paradigm that puts more emphasis on capital-intensive than labour-absorbing methods of production. It is thus recommended that for South Africa to achieve its sustainable development potential, it should consider a reorientation of the

Employment Status by Race and Gender, 1996 and 2003		Table 4
Percentage of Women	1996	2003
Black	51	55
Coloured/Asian	22	31
White	6	10
Percentage of Men		
Black	35	42
Coloured/Asian	14	24
White	4	6

Source Adapted from Statistics South Africa, 1996 October Household Survey and September 2000 and 2003 Labour Force Surveys.

Occupation by Race and Gender, 2003						Table 5
	Women %			Men %		
	Black	Coloured / Asian	White	Black	Coloured / Asian	White
Legislators, senior officials and managers	2	4	15	4	10	29
Professionals	3	3	14	2	4	14
Technical and associate professionals	11	12	20	6	9	15
Clerks	8	23	36	5	9	7
Service and sales workers	12	13	10	13	10	8
Skilled agricultural and fishery workers	4	0	1	4	1	3
Craft and related trades workers	5	5	2	19	20	17
Plant and machine operators and assemblers	3	8	1	19	13	4
Elementary occupations	27	20	1	27	25	3
Domestic workers	25	11	0	1	0	0
Total	100	100	100	100	100	100

SOURCE Adapted from September 2003 Labour Force Survey, Statistics South Africa, Pretoria.

Occupation by Race and Gender, 1995 and 2003							Table 6
	Women %			Men %			
	Black	Coloured / Asian	White	Black / Asian	Coloured	White	Total
Senior management and professionals							
1995	11	3	14	22	9	41	100
2003	12	5	18	20	11	34	100
Technical and associate professionals							
1995	30	5	16	22	5	22	100
2003	33	8	14	23	8	14	100
Clerks, service and sales workers							
1995	21	9	22	29	8	10	100
2003	28	12	15	32	7	6	100
Skilled production							
1995	8	3	1	55	14	19	100
2003	14	4	1	60	12	9	100
Elementary occupations							
1995	39	7	0	44	9	1	100
2003	37	6	0	45	10	2	100
Domestic workers¹							
2003	86	9	0	4	1	0	100
Total employees							
1995	23	6	9	39	9	14	100
2003	30	7	7	38	9	9	100

SOURCE Adapted from statistics South Africa. 1995 October Household Survey and September 2000 and 2003 Labour Force Surveys Note domestic workers are not aggregated separately from other elementary occupations in 1995

economy. This would mean, for example, changing the labour market structure from its historical exclusionary basis to one that specifically provides incentives for labour-absorbing modes of production.

According to Statistics South Africa of 2004, the unemployment rate for Black women was 55.9 percent and for Black men 40.1 percent, while for White women and men, the unemployment rates were 9.5 percent and seven percent respectively. Women who are employed are more likely to find lower paying employment. Moreover, women have less time available for employment, as they spend time on unpaid care work.

Unemployment is particularly high for young people. Black women under the age of 30 face an unemployment rate of 75 percent. They constitute 17 percent of the labour force – that is, the employed plus the unemployed – but 31 percent of the unemployed. Women are most likely to be engaged in subsistence work or support for family enterprises. Moreover, since Black women face the highest levels of unemployment, they are more likely to be discouraged from actively seeking paid work.

Income differentials appear largely to reflect the concentration of women in lower-paid industries and occupations. While unequal pay for equal work persists, it is illegal and generally camouflaged by differences in job title and status. In 2003, five percent of Black women were employed as managers and senior professionals, compared to 33 percent of White men. Some 25 percent of Black women were employed as domestic workers, and 27 percent were elementary (that is, "unskilled") workers.

Black women have, however, made little progress in occupational terms between 1996 and 2003. The share in senior management and in the professional category rose only from 11 percent to

12 percent in this period. In contrast, Coloured and Asian men and women gained substantially in this period, while the share of Black men reportedly declined.

Overall, between 1995 and 2003, Black women moved from the lower level professions – essentially nurses and teachers – to clerical and retail work.

As Figure 1 shows, changes over time emerged with generational differences. Black women under 30 are more likely to be unemployed and, if employed, to work in retail and clerical occupations. They are distinctly less likely to have jobs as teachers or nurses.

Women are predominantly found in relatively poorly paid sectors, as Figure 2 demonstrates. In 2003, half of all women were employed in domestic and sales work, which are poorly paid. Some eight percent were in farming, with the vast majority being subsistence farmers and farm workers. A further 17 percent were in education and health – sectors requiring considerable skills, but paying relatively little given the high education level.

There is a strong statistical correlation between the percentage of Black women in the labour force of a sector and the percentage of workers in the sector earning under R1,000. For Black women, domestic labour remains a critical source of paid labour. By 2003, some 96 percent of domestic workers were Black women. This is the worst paid industry, with 93 percent of workers earning under R1,000 a month.

Formal employment
There are nearly 10 million (9,583,771) people between the ages of 15 and 65 working in formal employment in South Africa. Of these 58 percent are male and 42 percent female, indicating a gender bias in formal employment. Table 7 shows that the profile of Black women's employ-

Women's Occupation by Age, 2003 — Figure 1

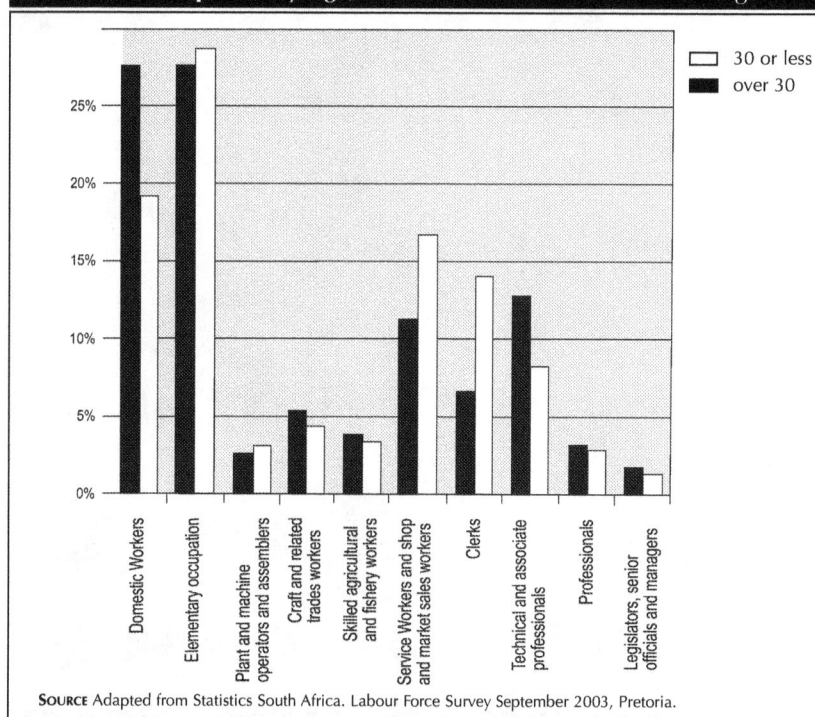

SOURCE Adapted from Statistics South Africa. Labour Force Survey September 2003, Pretoria.

Industry and Incomes by Race and Gender, 2003 — Figure 2

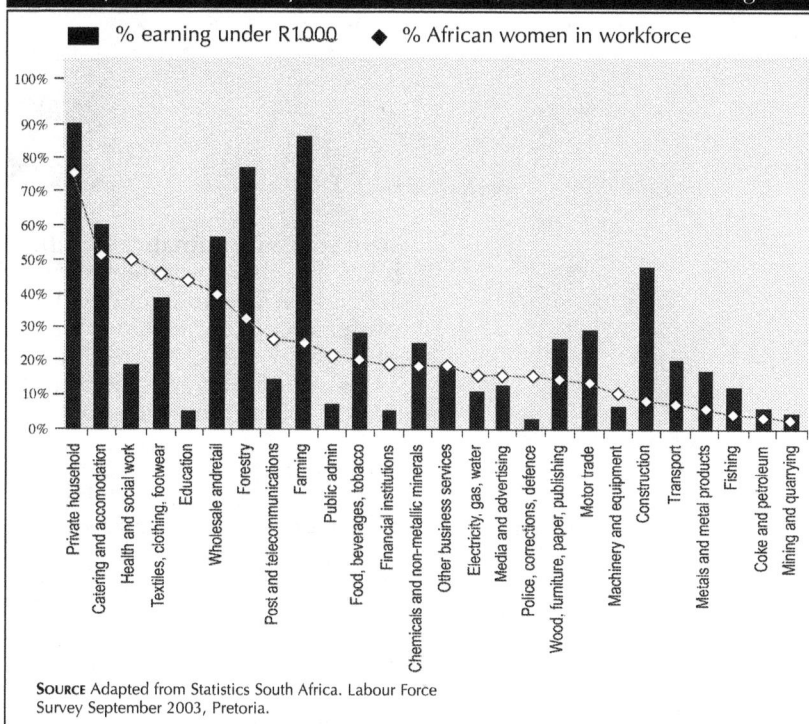

SOURCE Adapted from Statistics South Africa. Labour Force Survey September 2003, Pretoria.

Employment and Unemployment by Race and Gender, 2003							Table 7
	Women %			Men %			
	Black	Coloured / Asian	White	Black	Coloured / Asian	White	Total
% of population group							
Formally employed	20	44	53	34	49	52	33
Informally employed	10	3	4	12	5	3	9
Domestic worker	10	6	0	0	0	0	4
Unemployed	60	47	43	54	46	45	54
Total	100	100	100	100	100	100	100
% of employment grouping							
Formally employed	21	8	9	39	1	12	100
Informally employed	40	2	2	49	4	3	100
Domestic worker	86	9	0	4	1	0	100
Unemployed	38	6	5	37	7	7	100
Total	35	6	6	37	8	8	100

SOURCE Adapted from Statistics South Africa, Labour Force Survey September 2003, Pretoria.

Number of Senior Managers per Race Group					Table 8
	1995%	1997%	1999%	2000%	2001%
Black	11.0	19.1	20.5	23.2	23.5
Coloured	10.1	19.6	25.5	24.7	24.4
Indian	11.8	16.6	22.4	21.7	19.7
White	6.1	8.8	14.5	16.2	14.0
Total	7.9	13.0	17.5	19.9	19.0

SOURCE Public Service Payroll Information (PERSAL), 2002.

ment status is dramatically different from that of other groups defined by race and gender. They are far less likely to have formal jobs, and far more likely to be unemployed, informally employed, or domestic workers.

Women in the public sector
The current government inherited a public service where women were grossly under-represented in managerial positions. Changes for women in the public sector have been less impressive than the rate of transformation occurring in relation to women in parliamentary politics.

Although the Public Service has almost doubled its representation of women managers over a five-year period, it is still a concern that the retention rate for women is still poor due to gender-insensitive policies in the working environment.

Women in the private sector
In a study on *Gender and the Private Sector* done in 1999, the Comm-ission on Gender Equality indicates that the South African business community shows scant interest in promoting gender equality. This is despite the country's Constitution and statutory requirements obligating the private sector to address issues of inequality between men and women.[12]

The report documents the results of a survey of 103 companies within South Africa. Forty-seven percent of companies interviewed indicated that they did not have a gender policy and a significant number of companies indicated that they are not interested in this issue or that they are interested in business and employ people who can do the work. With respect to occupation levels, the report revealed that 59 percent of women in the sample were located in apprenticeship and trainee level jobs compared to 41 percent men.

Women in the informal and NGO sector
In contrast to women in the private sector, women are over-represented in the informal and NGO sector. The development sector is characterised by smaller staff complements as it generally has more flat structures than hierarchical structures. This often means that women have fewer opportunities for career advancement in this sector, than if they had been employed in the same position in the private sector. Smaller staff complements also often mean

heavier workloads and less time to pursue other career interests such as part time study.

This is especially so as women can generally not move vertically within a development organisation and have to either leave and work in another organisation or stay in the same position. In addition, the NGO sector work does not necessarily challenge the sexual division of labour, as development work is often perceived as being similar to work in caring and helping professions.

South Africa's non-profit sector is worth R14 billion a year and employs more than 600,000 people, making the sector's workforce larger than others such as mining, national government, transport, financial services and insurance.[13] However, according to national census figures released in 1998, South Africa's community, social and personal services sector was the largest employer in the country accounting for 1,350,249 of all employed people out of a total of 9,113,847.

The sector, including those in the public sector, constitutes 30.8 percent of all working people in South Africa.[14] This is an important sector for monitoring and evaluating transformation and change, not only because it is the largest employer, but also because it is a sector which often gives direction to changes in policy and is usually the sector closest to ordinary people and therefore most likely to effect change at grassroots level. Thus, one easy way of responding to different constraints facing women in economy would be for government to work closely with both private sector and NGOs in developing concrete initiatives with specific focus on women, more specifically at the grassroot level. In this regard, government has expressed its commitments in supporting such measures, as illustrated in Box 5.

Income and occupation inequalities

The high income and occupation inequalities in South Africa reflect the wider race and gender inequalities in society. They also indicate an economy in which insufficient people are economically active in areas that can make South Africa more competitive in the global economy. Reducing these inequalities is imperative for economic growth and South Africa has several programmes in place to do this. One important area of redress, skills development and the full utilisation of existing skills to ensure maximum productivity and efficiency can be found in government labour policies and legislation on employment equity and anti-discrimination.

Employment equity is a legal mechanism for addressing inequality within the formal sec-

---

Private sector still dominated by men   Box 4

A report released by the Employment Equity Commission in 2001 showed that women are inadequately represented across all sectors of the economy: at management level, 87 percent of all top management positions are still held by men and 80 percent of all senior management jobs are in the hands of men. Women currently hold 37.6 percent of jobs in management (all levels) and professional jobs combined – which includes the teaching and nursing professions. There are still many barriers preventing women from getting ahead in business. Besides lacking the necessary education and skills, they are often denied financial assistance without a male guarantor.

SOURCE Philippa Garson, www.southafrica.info/

Mbeki pledges to address economic empowerment of women   Box 5

President Thabo Mbeki on 10 May 2005 expressed concern over the efficacy of government's empowerment policies, particularly regarding gender-equality and the empowerment of women.

Speaking at the annual conference and first annual general meeting of the South African Women Entrepreneurs' Network (SAWEN), Mbeki said that while the government was to be commended on its equity and transformation policies and the passing of such acts as the Broad-Based Black Economic Empowerment Act, the Employment Equity Act and the Preferential Procurement Policy Act, he had, "doubts whether, in reality, these interventions were producing the intended results."

Mbeki singled out the issue of access to finance as a key obstacle faced by women entrepreneurs. Mbeki said that it was firstly the responsibility of government to ensure that its policies actually produce the desired results.

However, he added that it was also a responsibility of bodies such as SAWEN to, "exercise some oversight over what government is doing to facilitate the emancipation of women."

With a view to addressing the issue of gender (in) equality more accurately, a presidential working group on women had been formed and had already held its initial meeting.

Mbeki said that it was important that the President has systematic, regular discussions with the women of South Africa to determine the issues they face, hear their views on government's policy on women and, together, facilitate the implementation of strategies to fast-track the empowerment of women in South Africa.

SAWEN is an initiative of the Department of Trade and Industry (DTI's) Gender and Women's Empowerment. Since its establishment, SAWEN has provided members with business information and training through national workshops, supplied business-advisory services and interacted with government on its empowerment policies.

SOURCE http://www.miningweekly.co.za/min/news/today/?show=67092

tor and amongst those who already have jobs, or are seeking entry to jobs. The Employment Equity Act, 55 of 1998, seeks to provide equal opportunities within the workplace by providing protection against unfair discrimination, as well as requiring positive measures or affirmative action in favour of designated groups. Designated groups are those who have been and are excluded on the basis of race, gender and disability. Affirmative Action is specifically targeted at the redress of unemployment disadvantages experienced by these designated groups and ensuring their equitable representation in all occupational categories and levels in the workplace.

The Employment Equity Act requires employers to take positive measures and create plans to:
♦ Implement training measures and skills development plans;
♦ Improve access to jobs;
♦ Improve access to training and promotion opportunities;
♦ Advance all members of the workforce; and
♦ Progressively reduce dis-proportionate income differentials in the workplace.

Table 9 shows that in 2003 almost two-thirds of Black women earned under R1,000 a month, compared to three percent of White men.

Income by Race and Gender, 2003						Table 9
	Women %			Men %		
	Black	Coloured / Asian	White	Black	Coloured / Asian	White
Monthly income						
Up to R1000	64	31	5	40	23	3
R1001 to R2500	17	32	14	34	30	8
R2501 to R4500	9	18	27	15	22	14
R4501 to R8000	9	17	43	9	20	46
Over R8000	1	2	11	2	5	29
Total	100	100	100	100	100	100

SOURCE Adapted from September 2003, Labour Force Survey, Statistics South Africa, Pretoria.

Union membership

Overall, women are less likely to belong to unions than men. Within industries, union densities are lower for women than for men. Moreover, except for the social services, women generally work in less organised sectors, including domestic work and retail. As a result, in 2003, only 28 percent of women in formal and domestic jobs[15] belonged to a union, compared to 36 percent of men.

This situation makes it harder to enforce labour laws designed to protect workers. Labour legislation essentially depends on workers themselves and is organised in unions, to monitor minimum standards and ensure improvements through collective bargaining. The state itself does not have capacity to enforce standards by inspecting workplaces. Moreover, beyond some minimum requirements, it is risky for the government to set

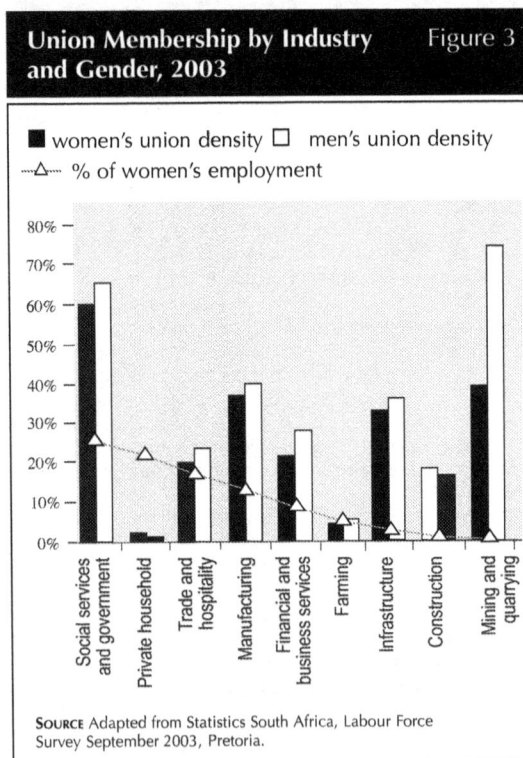

Union Membership by Industry and Gender, 2003 — Figure 3

■ women's union density □ men's union density
---△--- % of women's employment

SOURCE Adapted from Statistics South Africa, Labour Force Survey September 2003, Pretoria.

conditions of employment, since it cannot evaluate the economic circumstances facing individual enterprises.

This system means that where unions are weak, the laws become much harder to enforce. Workers must rely on responses to complaints they make to state inspectors, who are badly over-stretched. The Employment Equity Act requires employers to consult with workers on their equity plans; if unions are weak, this consultation is harder to design and less likely to mobilise strong worker inputs.

Women's working conditions[16]

Women's access to benefits and working conditions improved between 2000 to 2002. However, it is nonetheless substantially lower than that shown for males as a group. In 2002, 11.70 percent of women were workers for employers who contributed towards medical aid fund or health insurance, as compared to 15.5 percent for males. At least 57.7 percent females contributed to a pension fund/retirement fund in 2002, which is almost 10 percent more than that of males (i.e. 47.5 percent), which is an increase of 16.9 percent of females contributing to a pension fund from 40.8 percent in 2000 to 57.7 percent in 2002.

Part-time, casual and seasonal workers[17]

Global trends indicate that women are generally concentrated in casual, part-time and non-permanent jobs. Data obtained from the Census 2001 indicates similar trends for women in South Africa.

More males are employed as permanent workers. In 2000, the percentage difference between males permanently employed (i.e. 74.8 percent) as compared to women in the same group (71.9 percent) was 2.8 percent. In 2002,

this figure increased to 3.6 percent. While there was a gap between proportions of men and women being permanently employed, there was nonetheless an increase of 1.8 percent for females being permanently employed from 71.9 percent in 2000 to 73.7 percent in 2002.

The proportion of female workers who were employed as temporary workers was higher than that of male workers; at 14.3 percent women compared to 11.1 percent men in 2002. There was an increase of 0.6 percent in the number of women employed as temporary workers from 13.7 percent in 2000 to 14.3 percent in 2002. There was no significant change in the percentage of males employed as temporary workers from 2000 (i.e. 11.2 percent) to 2002 (i.e. 11.1 percent).

More women are employed as casual workers as compared to men. In 2000, 9.3 percent women were employed as casual workers as compared to 7.8 percent men; and in 2002, 7.2 percent women as compared to 5.7 percent men were casual workers.

In 2000, 1.04 percent women were seasonal workers compared to 0.7 percent males. In 2002, although there was a decrease in the numbers of seasonal workers, women (0.8 percent) still outnumbered men as seasonal workers (0.6 percent).

Self-employment and small, micro and medium enterprises (SMMEs)[18]

The ratio of males to females is closer in small and micro businesses as more women are involved in informal markets and are self-employed. In 2001, a Survey of the Employed and Self Employed showed that more women (2.7 percent), had small businesses, sold their goods to individual consumers; compared to 1.5 percent women with businesses that sold goods to other

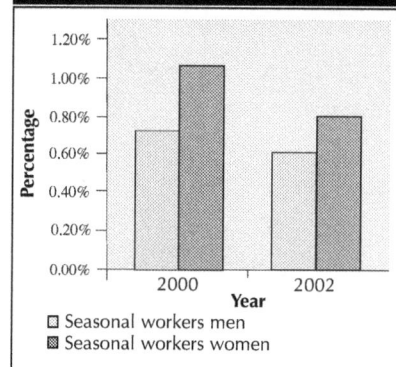

Seasonal Workers by Gender, 2000 and 2003 Figure 4

□ Seasonal workers men
▩ Seasonal workers women

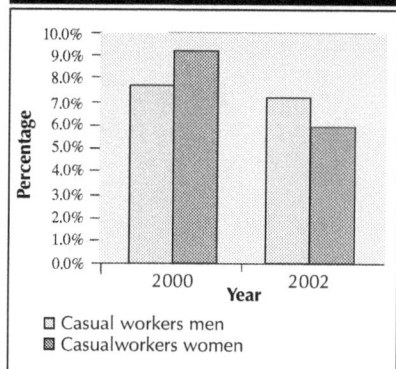

Casual Workers by Gender, 2000 and 2003 Figure 5

□ Casual workers men
▩ Casualworkers women

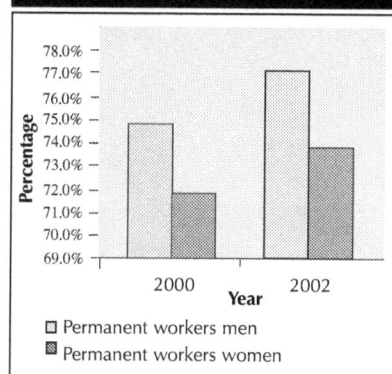

Permanent Workers by Gender, 2000 and 2003 Figure 6

□ Permanent workers men
▩ Permanent workers women

businesses. The lower figure for women entrepreneurs selling goods to other businesses indicates that fewer women own SMMEs with access to finances.

Challenges

Access to credit remains one of the major obstacles for women in trade. Understanding the market, through market research studies and analysis, is also another area of concern. Understanding the market also affects marketing and quality of products.

The minerals industry has been slow in implementing employment equity compared to other industries. There is scarcity of skills and resources for women to enter the industry in a meaningful manner.

Women must be given corresponding training to ensure that they are able to benefit from the programmes that are being put in place.

The key challenge for women-owned enterprises and SMMEs is sustainability. This is linked to access to funds and entry to and understanding of the market.

In the private sector, women are severely under-represented. Only 3.14 percent of all executives in the companies are women. Only 1.3 percent of the directors of the companies listed on the Johannesburg Stock Exchange are women.

There is severe under-representation of women in the private sector. The percentage of women in senior management levels is below five percent. Despite changes in some of the industries, the overall environment remains unfriendly to women.

Access to economic resources

In the past, women's survival strategies have been responsible for providing food, shelter, and education, amongst the poorest households, in the absence of employment and/or access to social assistance programmes. To the extent that they existed, women's enterprises were hampered by lack of access to information, access to credit, and/or savings.

Most women entrepreneurs were "un-banked" because banks were not geared to lend "low" amounts of money. Nor did they have any collateral to put up for any loans received. In some cases, women simply did not "enter" banks, as these institutions were "unfriendly."[19]

With the transformation process, government sought to amend policy guidelines for the Small and Medium Enterprises Development Programme to facilitate the entry of historically disadvantaged people, including women. In addition, the Black Economic Empowerment Strategy seeks to advance Black people, including women, within the mainstream economy.

Women entrepreneurs continue to rely on government, rather than the Financial Sector, for assistance in advancing their businesses.[20] For example, only 2.9 percent received assistance from commercial banks, as opposed to 9.8 percent men. In stark contrast 35.4 percent women received start up funds from government grants whereas 23.3 percent of the recipients of government grants were men.

Nonetheless, women, especially in rural areas, continue to borrow money from moneylenders (51 percent as opposed to 3.4 percent men). This indicates that access to credit remains a serious challenge to women, and by and large, the majority of women remain vulnerable to exploitation, in their attempts to access credit, with women in rural areas most at risk.

A specific recommendation by South African women with regard to availing financial (and other resources) to women's eco-

Access to Economic Resources for 2001 by Sex		Table 10
Access to Economic Resource	**Female %**	**Male %**
Proportion of owners of non-VAT-registered businesses who needed money to start their businesses and received a grant from the government	35.4	23.3
Proportion of owners of non-VAT-registered businesses who needed money to start their businesses and received a grant from non-government.	3.8	38.7
Proportion of owners of non-VAT-registered businesses who needed money to start their businesses and received a loan from commercial banks	2.9	9.8
Proportion of owners of non-VAT-registered businesses who needed money to start their businesses and received a loan from friends and relatives	84.8	79.9
Proportion of owners of non-VAT-registered businesses who needed money to start their businesses and received a loan from money lenders / *mashonisas*	5.1	3.4

Source Survey of the Employed and Self-Employed (SESE), Statistics SA, 2001.

nomic initiatives is the recommendation for the establishment of a special fund for women's projects.[21] The envisaged fund is to be a substantial one, with most women's groupings arguing that it should be at the level of the *Umsobomvu* Fund, which targets youth. Amongst the strong movers for the development of a national programme to support women entrepreneurs is the Women's Development Bank initiative, which noted in October 2001 that the Reconstruction and Development Programme of 1994 recommends that: "a specific programme must be established to ensure government support for women entrepreneurs. It must be easily accessible and include skills training and access to credit."[22]

Women's unpaid labour
According to a survey of time use in South Africa,[23] women spend more time on reproductive activities than men and are more likely to do the work of rearing and caring for children and fetching food, water and fuel. Men are more likely to be producing goods and services exchanged in the market. This is an indication that while women spend most of their time in household maintenance (which does not contain any monetary value) men spend most of their time on productive activities such as production of goods for sale which in turn put them in a better position both economically and financially, as well as earning them a high status in society.

Unlike men, women's roles in society are more often than not perceived within the tenuous duality of motherhood and economic dependence. Home-based tasks, childcare, collecting firewood and water, subsistence farming and taking care of other dependants are all tasks that are systematically omitted in the broad analysis of women's contribution to the national economy. The omission of such activities in the national statistics is an indication that the vital contribution of women in the economy is being sidelined. It is now important to recognise the important roles that women play and can play in growing, the South African economy and in creating jobs.

*Recognising
the participation
of women in
the economy
is important.*

Recognising the participation of women in the economy is important for government, as it forms part of the commitment to transform South Africa, away from a racially divided society and economy.[24] The low level of participation by women in the formal economy, as either small business owners or entrepreneurs, has for a long time been recognised as a problem in South Africa.

Constraints, which hamper women's ability to participate in the economy and become entrepreneurs consist of the regulatory environment, which includes government legislation, education, culture, limited access to management and job opportunities and family responsibilities. These inhibiting factors result in a number of difficulties for women entrepreneurs, such as getting adequate finance, having inadequate skills to start and manage a business, challenges in breaking into the marketplace for their products or services, risks of crime and violence, lack of access to information and often poor use and understanding of technology.[25]

Mining industry

Mining is the largest sector of the economy followed by manufacturing, oil and gas, chemicals, agriculture and tourism. The country has a variety of minerals and mineral products that are exported to as many as 87 countries. Each year, approximately 55 different minerals are produced from more than 700 mining facilities, with gold, platinum group elements, coal and diamonds dominating exports and revenue earnings. An assessment of the performance of the mining sector suggests that the sector is growing and attracting more foreign investors, hence contributing to the economic growth rate.

However, these developments contribute less towards addressing the entrenched gender inequalities, as the majority of the poor people, more specifically women have not been able to benefit from the overall economic growth.[26] Since the apartheid era, gender and race discrimination has remained a major hindrance towards equal redistribution of the national resources. For decades, women were almost excluded in the mining industry. In the post-apartheid era, the mining industry structures have been changing dramatically.

The change also flows from the introduction of South Africa's new Mining Charter that cedes all mineral rights to the State as well as introducing an empowerment component for all future mining developments in the country. This has resulted in the involvement of women in the sector, once exclusively dominated by men, and has given rise to the formation of the organisations such as South African Women in Mining Association (SAWIMA) and Technology for Women in Business (TWIB).

The TWIB was created under the auspices of the Department of Trade and Industry (DTI) in 1998, to help advance women in business, with a particular emphasis on the application of science and technology to achieve business growth in women-led enterprises. SAWIMA was launched in 1999 specifically to assist women who are formally and informally involved in mining. The association, among others, mobilises women miners to set up programmes to address the needs and interests of female miners. SAWIMA has, since inception, established a resource centre for women in mining and other activities aimed at promoting gender equality and women empowerment through capacity building training initiatives.

Women, clothing and textiles

The clothing and textiles manufacturing sector is advertised as one of the pillars of South Africa's economy, providing direct employment more than 200,000 people and indirect employment to around 500,000 people in total, including cotton farmers.[27]

Studies on this sector suggest that being labour intensive, clothing and textiles manufacturing industries have strong potential to create jobs for unskilled labour.[28] It is argued that if properly planned, the clothing and textile industry can be the largest employer of women in South Africa, especially those who do not have required skills and are unable to compete on the labour market. The participation of South Africa in the Western markets through the African Growth and Opportunity Act (AGOA), which permit duty-free entry of clothing and selected textiles,[29] is also said to be contributing to the advancement of the sector.

At the same time, this sector has been hard hit by globalisation, the reduction of trade tariffs and the consequent inflow of cheap clothing. In the past 10 years, 150,000 formal jobs have been lost, and another 4,000 in the first four months of 2005.[30] As a result, the sector has witnessed a re-organisation that has seen the retail clothing chains "increasingly organising the production of garments while at the same time driving a process of fragmentation, subcontracting and home-working in response to cheap imports."[31]

These developments negatively impact on the rate of women's economic empowerment in the sector, which has remained low. Due to the roles that women have historically played in the industry (as seamstresses, pattern cutters) which rates their labour in different ways from men's (machine operators, technicians), women textile workers are still far less remunerated than their male counterparts.

The general picture is that South Africa's economic growth in this sector has benefited men more than women. There is need to empower women through business training so that they can have access to AGOA markets. Because women form the majority of poor people in South Africa, supporting them to become more competitive in international business ventures will certainly have multiplier effects to meet MDGs and poverty eradication targets.

Women and agriculture

Agriculture plays a smaller and declining role in South Africa's economy than elsewhere in Africa. It contributes less than four percent to the country's GDP.[32] However, it is an important sector not only to the country's economy but also to the southern African region as it is a net exporter of food to other SADC countries.

Agriculture creates employment for more than a million people.[33] In terms of productive land, South Africa has about 15 million hectares, 12 percent of the land area under cultivation and about 10 percent of this is under intensive irrigation.[34]

The sector is well developed with 55,000 commercial farmers.[35] However, men dominate the commercial farming sector. Women are active in smaller scale farming, but often do not have the final control. When land becomes commercialised, control is often taken away from women.[36] Thus, men are still in charge of major agricultural production factors and the gendered division of labour and low status of women in society have resulted in very few women being involved in commercial agriculture and other planning functions in the agricultural sector. This is the case, even though in numerical terms, the majority of those active in farming are women.[37]

There is need to empower women through business training.

Men are still in charge of major agricultural production factors.

In addition, almost 54 percent of the South African population is located in rural areas,[38] of which an estimated 70 percent are poor or very poor.[39] Agricultural production is crucially important to the rural population, especially women. It is estimated that it is the third most important form of livelihood strategy in rural areas, after wage labour and state pensions.[40] From this point of view, women farmers' access to a range of benefits and services, including extension services that will assist them and their families to survive and develop productive capacity is vital.

There have been major policy changes in the agricultural sector. These include:

- Liberalising agricultural trade;
- Implementing land reform policies and programmes;
- Reforming institutions governing the sector; and
- Introducing a minimum wage for farm workers.

The country's strategic plan for agriculture clearly indicates that the medium-term goal for South Africa's agricultural sector is to generate equitable access and participation by providing security of tenure for present and future participants; equitable access to resources; promoting sustainable use of natural and biological resources; and creating a predictable and consistent policy environment. The Discussion Document on Agricultural Policy in South Africa states that "all programmes will be examined to ensure that women at least have equal access and that programmes are targeted at them."[41]

Agricultural Development is one of six programmes in the department of Agriculture. It aims to promote access to farm settlements, agribusiness, institutional and human resource support and agricultural communication for historically disadvantaged groups and individuals.

However, none of these areas specify women as historically disadvantaged and as yet, no policy for outreach to women exists.

One example of this can be seen in agricultural extension services, which have been directed primarily at men as beneficiaries. There is no specific policy on women's access to agricultural extension services, although this need is recognised.[42] An overall policy on gender in agriculture is in the process of being developed.[43]

Despite the policy gaps, there are several activities directed at women in the sector. In the National Department of Agriculture, these tend to focus primarily on access to capital and credit, access to markets, access to land and water and the issue of skills development, mentorship and training.[44] The gap between gender insensitive policies and particular programmes for women means that gender inequalities in agriculture tend to be addressed in an *ad hoc*, rather than holistic, manner. In so far as the country's strategic plan for agriculture seeks to increase wealth creation in rural areas and provide sustainable employment, it is important to ensure that these efforts are inclusive, that they involve women and do not underestimate their role and contribution in this sector.

A significant area of inequality in the agriculture sector lies in the situation of farm workers. A large proportion of rural people are farm workers. Studies show that women constitute the majority of these, but are more likely than men to be casual and seasonal workers and earn less than their male counterparts. A labour force survey carried out in September 2001 found that women's mean monthly wage[45] was R579 against R756 for men. In addition, women's rights are often ignored by their employers.

Access to land

There are particular distortions in South African land ownership that stem from colonialism and apartheid. In 1913, the Natives Land Act segregated Africans and Europeans. African farmers were able to farm only on the eight percent of land designated as reserve land. This had the dual effect of radically undercutting the competitiveness of African farmers and dispossessing most Black people of their traditional rights to land. As a consequence, land distribution in South Africa is one of the most unequal in the world. Policies on access to land have aimed at addressing the racial imbalances in land ownership and control in both rural and urban areas.

Within this overall racial inequality and exclusion, women, especially in the rural areas, have been excluded from rights to land. The inherited legislation on the allocation of land resources, combined with a patriarchal culture of male domination, have inhibited women's claims to property, residential rights and land use. These laws and customs particularly affected Black women in the rural areas where traditional authorities and male leaders still largely control the communal land. In addition, customs and customary practices excluded women from the right to own, inherit or profit from land.

Women are generally insecure in their rights to land. Their ability to access land usually depends on their relationships with men. Whether married, single, widowed or divorced, they often depend on the chief or headmen to make a decision about their rights of access and use. As a rule, women do not serve on the tribal structures and therefore are unable to influence decisions and are often not informed regarding subsidies and grants.

Single, divorced and widowed women are more disadvantaged. "Married women with children have the most advantages; followed by widows with grown children; then younger widows with younger children and the most disadvantaged are single women with children. Married women with absent husbands rarely have difficulty in accessing land but have little cash to develop land and little decision-making power."[46]

The majority of rural women live in communal areas. Tenure reform is the subject of the Communal Land Rights Act (2005) that recognises women's rights to land. However, it is argued that this is "textual rather than substantive." Particularly problematic is that it "also empowers reconstituted Traditional Councils (established under the Traditional Leadership and Governance Framework Act) to become the all-important land administration committees that would manage communal land once it has been formally transferred into community ownership."[47] This has resulted in a pending Constitutional Court challenge claiming that the Act "fails to satisfy the constitutional requirement for remedying tenure insecurity 'as a result of past racially discriminatory laws or practices,' including the gendered discrimination borne by black women."[48] Walker suggests that the Act "can be seen as the culmination of a decade in which the state has consistently tried to finesse rather than confront the inconsistencies in its twin-track approach to women's land rights, on the one hand, and traditional leaders' powers on the other."[49]

Land tenure rights have been particularly important for farm workers and women living on communal land. In relation to the former, tenure reform inherently has significant implications for

Land distribution in South Africa is one of the most unequal in the world.

the productive and residential rights of farm workers. However, it affects women differently, especially because employment is the primary basis on which occupiers acquire tenure rights. Women farm-dwellers are rarely considered as occupiers in their own right, but rather as secondary occupiers, whose tenure is dependent on the continued employment on the farm of their male partners.

Women with disabilities

Women with disabilities are often ignored when an assessment of women's position in society is made. The current Employment Equity Act of 1998 refers to people with disabilities as a homogenous group without specific reference to disabled women. Organisations and companies in their employment audits supply no disaggregated gender data. It is therefore necessary to point to the fact that women constitute about 52 percent of all people who have a "physical or mental handicap, which prevents the person from carrying out daily activities independently, or from participating fully in educational, economic or social activities."[50]

These disabilities are either physical, due to temporary or permanent injury or are a result of emotional trauma making an individual incapable of performing normal duties. Disability can also be the result of mental impairment, which makes the person unable to function in a work environment.

Disability within the family environment according to Sanders[51] has a different impact on women members. In many insta-nces, it is the woman (wife or mother) who takes on the caregiver's role. This adds additional functions, knowledge and in some instances even requires that the woman has to leave her paid job. If a woman becomes disabled, she remains the mother and wife in the family. If she receives a disability grant, she may even be perceived as the breadwinner.

The White Paper dealing with the Integrated National Disability Strategy 1997 acknowledged the fact that women with disabilities, and specifically Black women, are still marginalised and discriminated against by the existing patriarchal society. They are still seen as dependent, passive and needy. The White Paper further noted that an alarming high proportion of caregivers of disabled children are grandmothers, thus further exacerbating the disadvantaged circumstances of elderly women in South Africa.[52]

EDUCATION
Education status and trends

Education and skills development play a crucial part in the eradication of poverty. It has been the priority of the Education Department that the girl-child gets equal access and opportunity to education and to minimise the dropout rate among girls. For instance, special arrangements are made for the girl-child to attend school during and after pregnancy. The South African Schools Act of 1996 also makes it compulsory for all children to attend school for 10 years and states that there should be no discrimination between boys and girls.

South Africa has made significant progress since 1994 to ensure access to education for almost all children aged seven to 15. According to the Department of Education, the education system accommodates more than 12.3 million learners (50.5 percent women), 300,000 university students (54.6 percent women), and 190,000 Technikon students (45.5 percent women). As of the year 2000, there were more girls than boys enrolled in schools.

Emerging best practices

Across all levels advances have been made in the proportion of women in the education sphere with parity being achieved in almost all spheres. Additionally, there are noted increases in the participation rate of all children in education.

In 2001 the figures[53] for the girl- and boy-child between 0-17 years in the education system were equal. Additionally, the increase in the proportion of females under 19 years attending school has increased phenomenally from 21.33 percent in 1995, to 65.53 percent in 1999.[54]

Table 11 provides a detailed outline of the level of schooling attained by females compared to males aged 20 years and older.

Gender, race and education

The disparity between males and females in educational qualifications is still large. Twenty percent of Black females and 13 percent of Black males do not have any formal schooling, whereas only less than one percent of White females and males do not have any formal schooling.[55]

There are 4,567,497 people over the age of 20 years who do not have any schooling. Women account for 60 percent of this number. In South Africa, unlike many other developing countries, the number of women enrolled in educational institutions exceeds that of men. This is the case at the secondary school level as well as at tertiary level, the reason being the high dropout level of the boy child and the fact that it is easier for boys to get access to menial and unskilled work than girls.

Table 11 indicates that of the total number of people with no schooling (i.e. 4,567,497), there are 2,737,244 (i.e. 59.9 percent) women in this category as compared to 39.1 percent males. This shows that for every one male not

receiving schooling in the country, there are two females. In every other category indicated in the Table, however, there are more females than males receiving education. This is in keeping with the population profile of the country.

Women in general, and Black women in particular, tended to take degrees in "softer" subjects – education, culture, social and business studies. They remained poorly represented in the "harder" subjects like science and engineering, as well as in the professions (See Table 12).

Highest Level of Education by Sex among those Aged 20 and Over			Table 11
Level of Education	**Male**	**Female**	**Total**
No Schooling	1 830 254	2 737 244	4 567 497
Some Primary	1 958 814	2 124 928	4 083 742
Completed Primary	52 996	870 471	1 623 467
Some Secondary	3 697 317	4 148 808	7 846 125
Grade 12/Std 10	2 539 565	2 661 036	5 200 602
Higher	1 033 524	1 117 811	2 151 336
Total	**11 812 470**	**13 660 299**	**25 472 769**

SOURCE Census 2001, Statistics SA 2003.

Degrees by Field, Race and Gender, 2003					Table 12
		Percentage of degrees in field			
Field	**Total number**	**Men**	**Women women**	**Black men**	**White**
University degrees as % of total tertiary degrees	37	44	32	23	57
Tertiary ex university					
Soft subjects (education, social studies, culture)	549 000	27	42	47	11
Business and communications	360 000	22	25	21	22
Professionals (health, law, services)	279 000	14	21	19	18
Hard subjects (engineering, science, agriculture, construction)	342 000	37	12	13	49
Total	**1 531 000**	**100**	**100**	**100**	**100**
University degrees					
Soft subjects (education, social studies, culture)	296 000	22	44	49	13
Business and communications	248 000	30	24	21	33
Professionals (health, law, services)	202 000	22	23	22	19
Hard subjects (engineering, science, agriculture, construction)	172 000	26	9	8	35
Total	**918 000**	**100**	**100**	**100**	**100**

SOURCE Adapted from Statistics South Africa, Labour Force Survey, September 2003, Pretoria.

Moreover, the majority of Black graduates still attend historically Black universities, which employers considered to be of lower quality. Both these arguments, however, point to deeper institutional factors as a problem, rather than simply levels of education.

Tertiary level education

At tertiary level, figures indicate that women receiving tertiary education surpass men. Table 13 illustrates the levels of tertiary education received by women as compared to that received by men.

The percentage of females who are primary graduates exceeds that of males. The situation is the same for the proportion of females who are secondary graduates. However, the proportion of females who are university graduates is lower than that for males. In 1995, while there were 60.2 percent male university graduates, there were only 39.8 percent females. This figure increased in 2002 to 45.8 percent female university graduates, indicating an increase of six percent from 1995 to 2002. More males attend universities because of the outlay of finances to male education, regarded as a future investment for families, whereas females marry and leave the family homes, thus not contributing to income.

In keeping with traditional, global trends, the scenario is no different in South Africa with regard to the fields of study chosen by females. In 2002, 15.6 percent females graduated in health sciences and social services as compared to only five percent males. The health sciences and social service fields have been traditionally regarded as female-oriented in nature, reinforcing the belief that women are caregivers and nurturers by nature.

Whilst in 2002 only three percent females were graduates in the manufacturing, engineering and technology sectors, 19.7 percent males graduated in these fields. A similar trend can be identified in other traditionally male-dominated fields. For example, 2.6 percent females graduated in law, military science and security as compared to six percent males; 0.9 percent females graduated in agriculture and nature conservation as compared to 4.4 percent males; and 5.2 percent females graduated in physical, mathematical, computer and life sciences as compared to 7.1 percent males.

Women as educators

The field of education has been traditionally regarded as an area where women's "natural" nurturing and care giving nature is advantageous to the job. This trend is further confirmed when one looks at the scenario of female educators in the country. In keeping with this patriarchal line of view, statistics show that women educators are found in large numbers in the primary and secondary schools and furthermore, in lesser numbers than their male counterparts at management levels within these schools. The proportion of female educators who are associate professionals was 67.9 percent in 2003, compared to 60.9 percent male educators in this category.[56]

The situation however is reversed in higher educational institutions, where fewer women

Comparison of Tertiary Level Education According to Sex						Table 13
Indicator	OHS 1995		OHS 1999		LFS 2002	
%	Female	Male	Female	Male	Female	Male
Percentage of primary graduates who are female	54.2	45.8	53.3	46.7	53.2	46.8
Percentage of secondary graduates who are female	50.2	49.8	51.4	48.5	51.7	48.3
Percentage of university graduates who are female	39.8	60.2	43.7	56.2	45.8	54.2

SOURCE Statistics South Africa

educators are found, especially at the senior levels of professors and researchers. The proportion of female educators who are professionals is 30.9 percent, compared to 36.4 percent males in this category.[57] The proportion of female educators who are managers – for instance rectors, principals and heads of department – is 1.2 percent compared to 2.7 percent males.[58]

Even though the field of education is predominantly regarded as suitable for women because of their natural nurturing tendencies, they are nevertheless concentrated in the lower positions and the decision-making positions rest firmly in the laps of men.

Historically, female teachers have also been the most exploited and discriminated against. They have earned the least money. When they married, they were regarded as minors and also had to resign. The "marriage bar" laid the foundation of "causalisation of married women teachers." It implied that when a female teacher got married she had to resign, lose all her benefits and could not hold a permanent position. Their childbearing role is never recognised. The pension benefits they receive at retirement are less than those of their male counterparts. Male teachers enjoyed better conditions of service, such as higher wages – and married men received allowances. Men also stood a better chance to be promoted to such posts as principals and school inspectors.[59]

According to a GETT Report,[60] the primary school system also remains highly feminised. Women make up 73.5 percent of teachers in primary schools. Although the current education system attempts to be much more gender-sensitive and equitable, women are still not appointed into meaningful senior positions in school administration. This has an effect on their earning capacity

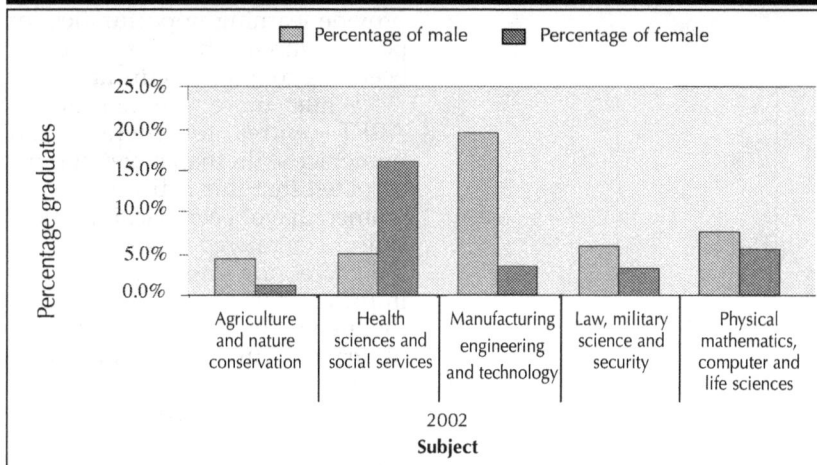

Percentage of Male and Female Graduates by Subject, 2002   Figure 7

that continues even to the age of retirement and beyond. Institutions increasingly favour men.

Women in higher education carry the burden of "gender", manifested as proportionally lower pay for equivalent work, poorer working conditions, and greater instability of employment, institutional sexism, overt and covert discrimination."[61] However, The Education White Paper (1997) stressed the importance of gender equity in institutions and the importance of building a supportive culture that promotes an equitable environment for women staff and students.

In an effort to improve education and training, it is imperative to create better employment opportunities for women in the teaching profession. The Department of Education has committed itself to the "creation of a high quality education system, characterised by accountability, transparency and efficiency."[62]

Adult basic education
The participation of adults, and in particular women in particular, in general, adult and further education and training has reduced the numbers of people with no school-

ing in the country. However, government has also introduced Adult Basic Education Centres (ABET) to provide learning opportunities for people who, in the past, have not been able to have an education.

While more women access ABET centres for literacy and numeracy skills than males, it must be noted that this is because more women have been lacking these skills as compared to men. Women are accessing opportunities to improve their skills and develop themselves. In 2002, the proportion of females attending adult basic education was 61 percent as compared to 39 percent males.[63]

Literacy rates
The literacy level for females in 2002 was 85.45 percent, compared to 89.64 percent for males.[64] This indicates that fewer women than men in South Africa are literate. In addition, literacy rates also vary according to race, due to the former system of separate education. In this regard, Blacks, and particularly Black women, tend to have lower literacy rates. A report in 1993 noted that whereas 99 percent of White women over 15 years had at least Standard six education, a third of all Black women in the Transkei had no education at all, with only 15 percent of this population having some form of secondary education.[65]

According to data[66] from the Census 2001, women in the age group 15 to 24 show the highest levels of literacy among literate women. This is as a result of the schooling received.

The proportion of women aged 25 to 44[67] who could read and write was 92 percent in 2002, compared to 93.9 percent men.

The proportion of women aged 45 and above who could read and write in 2002 was 70.4 percent, compared to 78.2 percent men.[68] Data indicated that the literacy levels for women in these age groups were steadily increasing[69] from 1999 (i.e. 91.5 percent and 68.5 percent

respectively) to 2002 (i.e. 92 percent and 70.4 percent respectively). This reflects the lack of access to education, in the past, by many women. Furthermore, the practice of keeping the girl-child at home to perform household chores has resulted in many females being illiterate.

CULTURE AND RELIGION
Cultural and religious norms can trap women in traditional gender roles. The South African Constitution recognises this by providing that cultural and religious rules and practices are subject to the Constitution, including the right to equality (section 30 and 31). It also provides for the codification of religious and customary law (section 15).

South Africa has enacted the Recognition of Customary Marriages Act, 110 of 1998, which removes inequality and discrimination against women in customary marriages. However, the situation with regard to customary inheritance remained discriminatory until the Constitutional Court declared the rule of primogeniture to be unconstitutional in the case of *Bhe vs Magistrate Khayalitsha*.[70]

Religious (Muslim) marriages remain unrecognised by law and the law reform process to codify these marriages has not reached finalisation. Women in these marriages can only resort to the courts to access rights that are not yet available to them, for example, to secure maintenance after the death of a spouse.[71]

Article 2(1)(b) of the Protocol to the African Charter on Human and Peoples' Rights on the Rights of Women in Africa calls for legislative measures to prohibit all forms of harmful practices that endanger the health and general wellbeing of women and girls. Harmful practices are defined as "all behaviour, attitudes and/or practices, which negatively affect the fundamental rights of women and girls, such as their right to

Fewer women than men are literate.

life, health, dignity, education and physical integrity."

There is evidence of ongoing harmful customary practices that discriminate against women. For example, the HIV and AIDS pandemic has seen the emergence of virginity testing of girls in KwaZulu Natal. This practice both exposes girls to abuse (by men who believe that having sex with a virgin will cure them of AIDS) and to ostracisation by the community as *izeqamgwaqo* or prostitutes.[72] The Commission on Gender Equality has criticised this practice as violating the rights to life, health and dignity of girls.[73]

The incidence of female genital mutilation, however, is unknown and views differ on the extent to which it occurs and as to whether it is a problem in the South African context.[74] Some questions have been raised about FGM, possibly occurring in some immigrant communities. It is also thought that forced marriage occurs in some communities.

The legal framework provides for the prohibition of such practices. For example, the Promotion of Equality and Prevention of Unfair Discrimination Act 4 of 2000, generally protects women against discrimination. Section 8 of the Act sets out a list of possible cases of unfair discrimination, each of which would need to be proved in terms of the Act. This section includes female genital mutilation,[75] gender-based violence[76] and "any practice, including any traditional, customary or religious practice, which impairs the dignity of women and undermines equality between women and men, including the undermining of the dignity and well-being of the girl-child."[77]

In theory, the Act covers practices such as female genital mutilation, forced marriages and virginity testing. However, these sections have not yet been tested in the courts and harmful practices tend to remain unchallenged.

POVERTY

Poverty has different meanings for different people or groups of people and can indicate lack of access to amenities or the lack of material ownership. In a recent Participatory Poverty Assessment,[78] different people identified poverty in a multifaceted way which included elderly without kinship and care, single mothers without kinship or partners, food insecurity where children in the household are malnourished or go hungry, overcrowded homes, the lack of basic forms of energy, where women have to walk great distances to collect water or fire wood in addition to being more vulnerable to physical attack and sexual assault, absent fathers, low paid jobs, unemployment and lack of job security.

Poverty is extremely gendered; women are more likely to be poorer than men. Poverty in South Africa also has a racial dimension; being concentrated among Blacks. Statistics show that 61 percent of Blacks and 38 percent of Coloureds are poor in comparison with only five percent Indians and one percent Whites.

Poverty also has a geographical dimension; being more prevalent among women in the rural than urban areas. This is because there are more female-headed households in the rural and peri-urban areas and these tend to have fewer adults working and the unemployment rate for women is higher than that for men. There is also a wage gap between women and men's incomes.

There are many indicators of poverty such as access to water, electricity and sanitation and these directly affect women's health. Girl-children from poor households are more likely than not to be kept out of schools to help with the household tasks, leaving less time for homework. Government has put in place sev-

Poverty is gendered and has a geographic dimension.

eral programmes to help women overcome poverty situations and these range from state pensions, social grants, public works programmes, programmes to improve access to quality housing and clean water amongst others. Table 14 shows access to pensions and grants by race.

Older women and poverty
Women tend to live longer than men, as shown by figures in Table 16. Older women will thus tend to have more years of life beyond the age when they are at the peak of their physical capacity and can be expected to support themselves. In addition, because women are less

likely than men to have earned during their younger years – and/or more likely to have earned less than men – they are more vulnerable to poverty in old age.

The old age pension has always – since the apartheid years – been amongst government's most significant poverty alleviation measures. Research over the years has shown that it is well targeted at women, Black people and rural people. Research has also shown that at least some of the pension is often used for supporting other people in the household, especially children. Further, some women still struggle to get pensions because of problems with identity documents, distance to pay points, etc. Yet, despite all these shortcomings, the impact of the old age grant on poverty levels on women is significant. Table 15 shows the distribution of the male and female beneficiaries of the old age grant across the nine provinces as at October 2003. The Table shows that women account for between 69 percent (Northern Cape) and 80 percent (KwaZulu-Natal) of the beneficiaries in each of the provinces.

This pattern suggests a significant bias in favour of women. One reason for this bias is that women qualify for the grant at the age of 60 years, while men qualify at the age of 64 years. Beyond this age cut-off, however, there is less bias in favour of women than one might expect, given that there is a means test for the grant and women are likely to be poorer than men. Table 16 shows the number of women and men in the age group covered by the old age grant. The Table reveals that women account for 71 percent of those who are eligible. The 75 percent in the previous Table differs only marginally from this. The grant is thus not unduly biased in favour of women given the eligibility criteria.

Share of Population Receiving State Pensions and Social Grants, 1996 and 2003 — Table 14

	% Black	% Coloured/Asian	% White
1996			
State pensions (includes civil service pensions)	15	13	8
Social grants	2	8	1
% earning under R1 000	**46**	**36**	**8**
2003			
State old-age pension	19	18	16
Disability grant	5	6	5
Child support grant	14	12	14
% earning under R1 000	**51**	**26**	**4**

SOURCE Adapted from Statistics South Africa, October Household Survey 1996 and Labour force Survey September 2003, Pretoria.

Beneficiaries of Old Age Grant by Sex and Province, October 2003 — Table 15

Province	Female	Male	Total	Female %
Eastern Cape	300 775	108 599	409 374	73.5
Free State	92 953	30 514	123 467	75.3
Gauteng	184 369	61 900	246 269	74.9
Kwazulu-Natal	333 588	86 117	419705	79.5
Limpopo	212 294	68 368	280 662	75.6
Mpumalanga	106 226	37153	143 379	74.1
North-West	126 270	50 748	177 018	71.3
Northern Cape	30 418	13 215	43 633	69.1
Western Cape	113 226	44107	157 333	72.0
Total	**1 500 119**	**500 721**	**2 000 840**	**75.0**

SOURCE Poggenpoel & Oliver, 2004: 25

Elderly Population Table 16 qualifying for the grant by Age Group and Sex, 2001			
Age group	Male	Female	Total
60-64		620 784	620 784
65-70	304 763	483 164	787 927
71-74	232 547	398 922	631 469
75-79	136 436	231 101	367 537
80-84	90 835	180 111	270 946
85+	45 907	111 425	157 332
Total	810 488	2 025 507	2 835 995
	29%	71%	100%

SOURCE Statistics South Africa, 2002b: 27-29

Generally, government's anti-poverty programmes have been hampered by worries about cultivating a culture of dependency. In particular, the housing, infrastructure and land programmes increasingly insisted that unless they were destitute, beneficiaries must contribute to costs. Obviously, this type of co-payment approach hits women hardest, since they tend to have the lowest incomes. When a co-payment programme was introduced in the housing programme in the early 2000s, it led to a severe slowdown in delivery. Most eligible households simply could not afford the down payment. After 2000, government ameliorated this policy by requiring that municipalities provide free minimum services for households with incomes under R800 a month.

In short, while government substantially improved access to basic services between 1994 and 2003, its efforts did not go far enough to overcome the marginalisation of most poor households. In particular, they did not raise incomes substantially in the former homeland areas. For each of the five services measured, those living in male-headed households are noticeably more likely to have access. Because – as noted above – a larger proportion of female than male heads have no formal education, their disadvantaged position affects a larger proportion of them.

Female-headed households[79]
In 1996, there were 5,216,205 male-headed households and 3,184,743 female-headed households.

The corresponding figures for 2001 are 6,837,160 and 4,933,112 respectively. This indicates that female-headed households have increased by 1,748,369 from 1996 to 2001.

Out of the total number of female-headed households for 2001, (i.e. 4,933,112), 3,330,297 (i.e. 83 percent) Black female-headed households recei-ved low annual incomes (i.e. R19,200 or less), as compared to 26 percent White female-headed hou-seholds, 53 percent Coloured female-headed households and 34 percent Indian female-headed households. Black women, many of whom are based in rural areas, are thus experiencing poverty levels in high numbers.

Furthermore, in 2001, 76 percent of female-headed households received low incomes as compared to 57 percent male-headed households, making women the poorest of the poor. Within each population group, more female-headed households receive low incomes as compared to their male counterparts. The highest percentage is indicated for Black female-headed households (i.e. 83 percent) as compared to 71 percent for Black male-headed households. The data, however does not address the growing phenomenon of child-headed households, especially the girl-child, who has to support the family as a result of the death of parents, especially through HIV and AIDS.

Women and public works
Public works programmes deliberately target women, therefore women's participation is significant. The motivation for doing this is that there are fewer job opportunities for women in the labour market and women tend to be poorer than men. However, disparities in occupations do exist.

Whilst providing jobs for women is commendable, the types and levels of jobs, as well as whether it is unskilled or skilled, at supervisory or management level and amount of remuneration are important indicators to monitor. In a study conducted by Mullagee and Nyman (2000), it was shown that women accounted for a smaller proportion of the 34 percent semi-skilled, 32 percent supervisory and 40 percent managerial positions in a Water for Work (WfW) programme. Women made up the majority of unskilled workers, and thus fell within the lowest wage bracket. What this reflects is that while the 60 percent target is commendable, it is not enough. To address this imbalance, the WfW programme has identified a target of 60 percent of the wages going to women because there is an imbalance in the gender composition in higher paid positions.[80]

Table 17 reflects the gender of the workers of three contractor teams of the Tsitsikama Water Project and shows that at a senior level, women do hold contractor and foreperson positions. In the team itself though, women hold the least skilled jobs, as herbicide applicators and labourers, even though they are in the majority.

Access to basic services

Substantial progress has been made since 1998 in extending basic household services, especially in the early 2000s, as Table 18 shows.

Often, however, these services were provided at a very low level,

and sometimes at unaffordable costs. Thus, new electricity connections to poor households generally sufficed only for light, not for cooking or for refrigeration. That ruled out cooking and *spaza* shops as a way to make money.

Housing

The quality of lives can be ascertained from people's access to and utilisation of services in respect of housing, energy sources, water access and usage as well as the ability to acquire household goods and access to communication technologies. In South Africa, the right to housing is entrenched in the 1996 Constitution, which states that: "Everyone has the right to adequate housing. The state must take reasonable legislative and other measures, within its available resources, to achieve the progressive realisation to this right" (Sections 26 (1) and (2).

In accordance with these rights, government has embarked on a series of laws, policies and mechanisms to provide access to accommodation and permanent housing. Initially the Reconstruction and Development Programme (RDP) set a goal of 300,000 houses per annum to alleviate the dire need to proper housing for the majority of the people. It also planned to provide one million low-cost housing within the first five years of democracy.

In accordance with the provisions of the Constitution, the Housing Act of 1997 was passed to promote amongst others, the active participation of women in housing. The Act also created the opportunity for women to actively participate in the industry itself by availing the opportunity to access grants for bridging finance.

Kehler's study in 2002 pointed out that 71 percent of all housing loan applicants in South Africa were women, while men only constituted 29 percent. It fur-

Gender Dissagregation Table17 of Jobs in a Public Works Programme		
Job	Male	Female
Contractors	3	3
Forepersons	1	1
Chain saw operators	3	0
Brush cutters	2	0
Herbicide applicators	1	8
Labourers	3	10
Total	13	22

SOURCE Sadan Mastoera-Workers interviewed 2004.

Access to Basic Infrastructure, 1996 and 2003				Table 18	
	Percentage of households with access to service			Average annual increase in share with access	
Type of infrastructure	1996	2000	2003	1996-2000	2000-2003
Electricity for lighting	64	71	79	2.1	3.6
Electricity for cooking	51	51	59	0.0	5.0
Piped water	82	83	86	0.3	1.2
Flush toilet	52	54	57	0.6	1.6

SOURCE Adapted from Statistics South Africa, 1996 October Household Survey and September 2000 and 2003 Labour Force Surveys, Statistics South Africa, Pretoria.

ther noted that 49 percent of women beneficiaries were working in the formal sector.

Statistics South Africa Census in Brief 2001, showed that more Black heads of households, (77 percent), were living in private shacks compared to White heads of households for instance (12 percent). When the extent of poverty and unemployment for women is taken into consideration, as well as the existing patriarchy that still favours men to women, the need for service delivery for women should take priority.

Government also divided the responsibility of the provision of housing amongst its three spheres:

+ National government: being responsible for establishing government structures and facilities to ensure sustainable housing development;
+ Provincial government: being responsible for the provision of an enabling environment for the development of housing; and
+ The municipalities: were made responsible to ensure that the right to adequate housing, the corresponding services, land and infrastructure is available.

A subsidy scheme has been established to ensure that the poor and dispossessed have access to proper housing. These subsidies are subject to certain criteria, which include:

+ That the combined income of the household does not exceed R3,500 per month. This amount has been contested by labour and trade union movements who have argued that the amount should be decreased to R1,500 per month, to ensure that the most needy benefit from the scheme;
+ Only permanent South African citizens or residents qualify for these subsidies;
+ A person should be legally competent (over the age of 21 and sound of mind);

+ The beneficiary should be married, co-habiting or single with dependents;
+ One should be acquiring a house for the first time; and
+ Has not received a subsidy previously.

The report on the implementation of the government program-mes shows that women received 49 percent of these grants; accounting for seven to 8.5 million of the people given shelter since 1995. The number of houses completed during the same period amounted to 530,602, which is much lower than the anticipated 300,000 per year.[81]

It is estimated that at least another two to three million houses need to be built to meet the need. The housing backlog has increased from 178,000 to 208,000 per annum. "Although there was a seven percent increase in the number of households living in formal dwellings, at least 4.1 million households are living in informal, traditional or backyard dwellings." [82]

As Table 19 shows, subsidised houses in the urban areas were substantially more likely to be distant from basic amenities, including clinics, schools and welfare offices. That in itself added to the time women had to spend to obtain services for themselves and their children.

Distance of Urban Subsidised Housing from Amenities, 2003 Table 19						
	Clinic (%)	Hospital (%)	Primary School (%)	Secondary School (%)	Welfare Office (%)	Postal Services (%)
Up to 30 minutes	84	60	92	86	70	78
with subsidy	87	66	94	90	78	84
without subsidy 30 minutes to an hour						
with subsidy	14	32	8	14	27	20
without subsidy	12	30	6	9	21	15
60 minutes or more						
with subsidy	2	8	0	1	3	2
without subsidy	1	4	0	1	1	1

SOURCE: Adapted from September 2003 Labour Force Survey, Statistics South Africa, Pretoria.

Housing by Type, 1996 and 2003			Table 20
Type of housing	Percentage of total		
	1996	2003	% Change
Formal over three rooms	54	50	24
Formal three rooms or less	15	26	126
Informal	12	13	42
Traditional dwelling	19	12	-18
Total	100	100	34

SOURCE Adapted from Statistics South Africa, October Household Survey 1996 and Labour force Survey September 2003, Pretoria.

Access to Services by Sex of Head of Household		Table 21
Services	% of Male	% of Female
Access to clean water	37	30
Access to sanitation	76	72
Electricity as main fuel for cooking	18	14
Electricity as main fuel for lighting	35	31
Access to refuse removal	25	20

SOURCE Africa et al, 2002.

Although the government subsidised over a million houses after 1994, progress was less impressive in terms of improving housing, largely because of substantial rural-urban migration. The share of informal housing remained virtually stable at 13 percent, formal housing expanded from 69 percent to 76 percent, and traditional housing declined.

A particular problem with the housing programme was that, largely due to the need to reduce the costs of land, most new settlements were located far from economic centres. As a result, they reduced access to economic opportunities and employment.

Water
The delivery of adequate and affordable services can form the basis for women's empowerment. Access to water in the household will increasingly relieve the burden and time spent on fetching water and assumes that more time could be spent on income generating tasks. Almost 40 percent of Black women in the former homelands, or 13 percent of all women, spent over an hour per week fetching water.

By 1999, 61 percent of the 11 million households countrywide still did not have running tap water inside their dwellings. Twelve percent of Black rural households still relied on flowing water, streams, wells and springs. Ten percent of people in non-urban areas and one percent in urban areas had to travel at least one km per day to fetch water. On average, the chore took them around five hours a week. Some 25 percent of Black women in the former homelands spent a similar amount of time, on average, fetching wood.

Sanitation
The National Sanitation Task Team, 2001 indicates that women and the elderly are the most inconvenienced by lack of toilet facilities. Communal facilities are seldom hygienic and privacy and dignity is often compromised. There is generally inadequate disposal of waste resulting in increased risk to personal safety and security.

Rural electrification
The poorest households, invariably headed by women in the rural areas, cannot afford electricity. Rural electrification has also been slow, making the burden to provide household fuel, usually a woman's and girl's duty, difficult. Access to electricity in the household will increasingly relieve the burden and time spent on fetching wood. Cooking on firewood makes women and girls more susceptible to pneumonia and other respiratory infections because of indoor pollution.

According to the Department of Minerals and Energy, women can spend up to five hours per day collecting wood. The time spent on collecting wood, fuel or dung can be spent on other economically viable functions such as looking for paid employment or creating a small business at home, if women had access to electricity. In some areas, access to electricity and water allowed women to open sewing-centres, hairdressing businesses, pre-schools and day-care centres.

Although there was an increase in the connections of electricity from 32 percent to 70 percent by 2001, it was found that only 49 percent of poor households used electricity for heating purposes.[83]

HEALTH
Conventionally, women's health has been explored solely in relation to their access to primary healthcare and their physiological well-being. Yet, much gender research has adopted a more holistic approach to women's

health – one that takes into account women's emotional and psychological wellbeing, their physical security and bodily integrity.

This understanding of women's health requires that "health" be explored in relation to a range of determinants and structural forces, which include women's socio-economic status and their location within traditional patriarchal institutions and relationships. From this perspective, women's health can be measured in relation to all facets of their public and domestic lives. Thus, access to healthcare as well as the development of health-seeking behaviour is interlinked to poverty.

Health care

The healthcare system in South Africa has been drastically reformed since 1994. Primary healthcare has become the focus, with clinics and health centres that are community-based being set up. Prior to 1994, the public healthcare system was primarily tertiary, hospital-based, and these facilities were all in the major cities. Healthcare was not particularly focused on universal access by the poor.

Although there has been notable progress in the provision of universal healthcare, there are still continual disparities in illness and death experienced amongst the Black and White populations in South Africa. The legacy of apartheid, the slow progress of reform as well as the influence of globalisation has affected the redress of inequities in the country.

Since 1994, more than 700 clinics have been upgraded or built. New mobile clinics have also been introduced. The state is responsible for providing services to more than 80 percent of the population.

However, in spite of progressive legislation and measures taken to make healthcare more accessible, challenges remain. The high levels of poverty (71 percent in rural areas and 50 percent overall) and 38 percent unemployment make it difficult for poor people to access health services.

Preventable diseases such as AIDS, tuberculosis, and cholera are the biggest challenges to the South African healthcare system. Staff shortages and inadequate outpatient care, especially in the rural areas; contribute to the fact that the primary healthcare service is still inadequate.

There has been a decrease in medical personnel in the public sector since 2000. In 2001, there were 19.8 medical practitioners per 100,000 population compared with 21.9 in 2000.

For professional nurses, the ratio reduced from 120.3 in 2000 to 111.9 in 2001. The nursing profession remains in essence a "woman's career." There are more than 30,000 vacancies for trained nurses in South Africa. According to the South African Nursing Council's records, there are just over 10,000 students in training.

The decrease in the nursing staff can be partly ascribed to the fact that government has cut back the budget for training and reduced the number of training colleges for nurses. The private medical sector has been training nurses for more than 10 years.

The private sector offers more benefits and opportunities to their nursing staff and this is in direct competition with the public health sector. Both the private and public sectors also compete with the overseas market that recruits professional nurses from the country.

Barriers to proper health care

Many women are still unaware of certain health threatening conditions and have not fully developed effective health-seeking behaviour. Contributing factors

HIV and AIDS pandemic is shortening the reproductive lifespan.

include long distances from the clinics and prohibitive costs of transport, especially in the rural and peri-urban areas, poor patient records which makes it difficult to maintain a continuity of care, long queues and staff shortages among others.

Reproductive health

The apartheid policies on urbanisation and the creation of the "homelands" have created wide provincial disparities in health, education and socio-economic indicators. This also translates to widely disparate levels of fertility across the country. It is difficult to make any comparative statistical analysis of the fertility rate amongst Blacks due to the fragmented and inadequate population statistical records of the past.

The fertility rate is defined as the average number of children born live to a woman during her childbearing age, which is 15 to 49 years of age. The importance of tracking fertility rates lies in the fact that the fewer children women have, the more likely they are to seek access to opportunities that will provide them with more rights and equality. South African women are likely to have fewer children than in the past or compared to other women in the region. This is likely to be the outcome of a number of factors, among them, declining fertility rates that are becoming a feature of developing countries.

In addition, women with HIV and AIDS have lower fertility rates, caused by secondary sterility and increased foetal deaths resulting from the virus. The HIV and AIDS pandemic is shortening the reproductive lifespan of many women, especially those in their mid-30s through opportunistic infections.

According to the Department of Health's report into maternal mortality, 82 of 565 maternal deaths in 1998 were recorded as being due to HIV and AIDS, and of these, women who (nearly three quarters of whom were less than 30 years of age) constituted more than 87 percent, had less than three deliveries.

Because of South Africa's history of widely accessible family planning services and health services that are well established, relative to the situation in sub-Saharan Africa, the low fertility rate can also be explained by the high use of contraceptives.

The 1998 South African Demographic Health Survey revealed an almost universal knowledge of at least one contraceptive method. Three-quarters of all women interviewed indicated that they used a contraceptive method at some stage during their lives while 61 percent of sexually active women reported that they were currently using modern contraception methods. By 2000, at least 66 percent of urban-based sexually active females and 53 percent of rural-based sexually active females used contraceptives.[84]

The Bureau for Market Research also provides estimates for births over the 25-year period 1996 to 2021.[85] These figures suggest that the birth rate will decline from 1,116,011 live births for the five-year period 2001-2006 to 949,035 live births for the period 2016-2021.

Increased urbanisation is also contributing to the decline in birth rate, particularly since the end of the policy of influx control has already resulted in smaller households and the increasing demise of the extended family in favour of a nuclear family arrangement. The average household size is 3.8 persons.

Coloured and Indian communities on average have bigger households than the rest of the population, with household sizes of 4.3 and four respectively. Whites with 2.8 persons per household have the smallest and

Black households have an average size of 3.8. Teenage or adolescent pregnancies are very high. One-sixth of the more than 26,000 children born to Black women were to women aged less than 20 at the time of birth.

Other factors that may contribute to the decline in the fertility rate are higher levels of education and access to legal abortion, among others.

Antenatal care

There is a very high utilisation (i.e. 94 percent) of antenatal care for births, according to the Demographic and Health Survey, 1998. This figure is slightly higher than the 89 percent observed in the Household survey[86] on inequalities in health conducted in 1994. Only three percent of the births in the period used in the survey received no antenatal care. This is a marked improvement from the 1988-1992 figures of 12 percent women who did not receive antenatal care recorded in the HSRC Survey.

Furthermore, there was a shift in the provider of antenatal care. The South African Demographic and Health Survey found that most women were seen by a nurse or midwife (66 percent) and fewer by doctors (29 percent). The HSRC survey showed that most women were seen by a doctor (59 percent) and that nurses (35 percent) saw fewer. A similarly low proportion of births were reported to have received care from a traditional birth attendant (less than two percent) in the 1988-1992 survey.

These results suggest that antenatal care services have become more accessible in the last 10 years.

Maternal mortality

Maternal mortality is associated with women's ability to access affordable maternity services, receive quality antenatal care and give birth safely. As indicated above, South Africa generally has high levels of utilisation of antenatal care and of giving birth within an institution. According to the South African Demographic and Health Survey (SADHS), 95.1 percent of women attended antenatal care at least once in their pregnancy and 83.7 percent of women give birth in an institution. However, these national figures hide deeper inequalities, with over 40 percent of very poor women in the rural Eastern Cape giving birth at home. Part of the reason for this is poverty, accessibility and affordability of transport.[87]

The maternal mortality ratio based on the South African Democratic Health Survey data is 150 maternal deaths per 100,000 live births for the approximate period 1992-1998.[88] Maternal deaths during this period account for about five percent of the total number of deaths in women of childbearing age.

The main causes for maternal mortality[89] as reported in the *Saving Mothers* Report on Confidential Enquiries into Maternal Deaths include hypertensive diseases of pregnancy (20 percent), infections including AIDS (18 percent), obstetric haemorrhage (14 percent), early pregnancy loss (12 percent), pre-existing maternal disease (11 percent) and pregnancy-related sepsis (9 percent).

"Since 1994, there has been strong political support for the improvement of maternal mortality, and important policy and programme developments for reducing maternal deaths. However, implementation remains a major stumbling block with maternal deaths remaining high, many of which have avoidable causes, and known and affordable solutions."[90]

Maternal death was made a notifiable condition in 1997. In the same year, a National Committee for Confidential Enquiries into Maternal Deaths (NCCEMD) was appointed to

Human rights/ social justice factors impact on maternal health.

The Constitution recognises the right to make decisions on reproduction.

advise the Department of Health on addressing this problem. The NCCEMD was asked to review maternal deaths in South Africa and then propose recommendations, which would assist in decreasing its incidence. The recommendations of the Committee are contained in a comprehensive Report.[91]

A limitation of the South African approach, which is similar to that of other UN Member States, is that it does not take into consideration human rights/social justice factors which impact on maternal health. More recent approaches to maternal mortality draw on more comprehensive human rights driven approaches to development. This human rights approach would see maternal death as a "social injustice" and recognise that many of the factors that impact upon maternal health result from women's poor status in society. "Despite the emphasis on women's rights in the early health policy frameworks, this has not found its way fully into a comprehensive policy framework on reducing maternal mortality."[92]

Fertility[93]

The most recent data available in this regard is from the survey conducted for the South African Demographic and Health Survey, 1998. The fertility indicators reported below are based on the answers provided by women aged 15-49 years regarding their reproductive histories.

The total fertility rate for South Africa, calculated from the 1998 South African Demographic and Health Survey data for the three-year period prior to the survey (roughly 1995-early 1998), was 2.9. The fertility rate tends to decrease with an increase in educational levels of women.[94]

Fertility rates[95] in urban areas were 2.3 and were substantially lower than in rural areas, which

were 3.9. This lower fertility rate in urban areas was apparent among all age groups.

Contraception

The Constitution recognises that the right to security of a person includes the right to making decisions concerning reproduction. Women also have the right of access to reproductive healthcare. This frames government policy on contraception.

The Health Sector Strategic Framework (1999-2004) addresses reducing teenage pregnancy and improving women's health as core health priorities.

In 2002, the government launched its National Contraceptive Policy Guidelines after a two-year consultation process. This policy moves away from a "population control" approach to an approach that focuses on increasing women's access to quality health services and emphasises choice. These Guidelines set out three policy objectives:

- To remove barriers that restrict access to contraceptive services;
- To increase public knowledge of client's rights, contraceptive methods and services; and
- To provide high quality contraceptive services.

Knowledge of contraceptive methods

Knowledge of contraceptive methods has been recognised, as a key factor in the uptake of contraceptives and lack of information is an important reason for unmet need. Women who know about a range of contraceptive methods are more likely to use a method.

The SADHS (1998) reports that 97 percent of women had heard of at least one modern method. This included women who were currently married, sexually active unmarried women and women who had no sexual experience. The survey further reported that knowledge of at least one method of contraception was equally high in both the married and the sexually active unmarried groups but slightly lower in the group of women with no sexual experience (86 percent). [96]

Contraceptive prevalence rate

Contraceptive use is an important reproductive health indicator. The 1998 SADHS found that three-quarters of women of reproductive age had used a contraceptive method, while nearly two-thirds (62 percent) currently use some form of contraceptive. The injectable contraceptive was the most common method. There were considerable age, race and socio-economic differences in access to and type of contraception used.[97]

The SADHS[98] also notes that contraceptive use is higher among currently married women (56 percent) and highest among women who were sexually active (62 percent). The highest prevalence was recorded in the 20-24 age groups, where 69 percent of all sexually active women were using a method of contraception. The report states that the rates drop to 57 percent in the 40-44 age group and to 46 percent among those 45 and over.[99] The survey also found that there was a large difference in contraceptive use between urban and non-urban women, with two-thirds (67 percent) of women in the urban areas using a method, compared to 54 percent in the non-urban areas.[100]

Education appeared to play a major role in contraceptive use with only a third (35 percent) of those who have not attended school using a method, compared to over three-quarters (79 percent) who attained a minimum of Standard nine.[101]

The Survey also found that White and Asian women reported the highest use (76 percent for White women and 80 percent for Asian women), compared to 59 percent of Black women and 69 percent of Coloured women. There were also differences in use between urban and non-urban Black women, with contraceptive prevalence higher in the urban areas.[102]

Abortion

Abortion is legal and free of charge in most state hospitals in South Africa. This has made life easier for women who opt to terminate pregnancy. The Choice of Termination of Pregnancy Act allows all women access to termination of pregnancy under certain circumstances. The Act aims to ensure that the rights of women are protected, and also to reduce health risks usually associated with illegal abortions.

Infant and child mortality rate

South Africa has a high Infant and Child Mortality rate, with higher mortality rates in non-urban areas. Whilst the high mortality figures are of concern and impact negatively on women, whatever the sex of the infant/child lost, it is significant to note that there is a higher percentage of mortality of boys. The pattern for higher mortality of male children than female children is an international phenomenon. The infant mortality rate, as per the South African Demographic and Health Survey, 1998, is 35.3 percent for females as compared to 49 percent for males. The Child Mortality rate as per the same survey is 13 percent for females as compared to 17.7 percent for males.[103]

It was found that, in South Africa, the mortality of infants and children is consistently higher in non-urban than urban areas. This is also true of Black rural residents compared to their urban counterparts.[104]

The Act aims to protect the rights of women and reduce health risks.

Immunisation coverage of the girl-child[105]

In general, 63 percent of children aged 12-23 months were fully immunised against the basic childhood diseases, with a small differentiation between males and females; 62.2 percent being female and 64.7 percent male children. There is a lower percentage of girl-children receiving complete vaccination. Children from urban areas have slightly higher coverage rate (67 percent) than non-urban children (60 percent).

HIV and AIDS

The Department of Health estimates that by the end of 2001, about 4.74 million or one in nine South Africans were HIV-positive.[106] In 2001, more women (56 percent) than men were living with HIV and AIDS. This manifests itself in HIV-prevalence peaking not only in younger age cohorts for women, but also amongst women over 35 years. Black women are currently particularly affected. The roots of this vulnerability are complex. While physiology affects women's greater risk of HIV infection, this is compounded by women's lower socio-economic status and discriminatory cultural practices. At the core, is women's lack of autonomy and control over their sexuality in sexual relationships. Women are especially impacted by cultural norms relating to gender, which are often enforced by violence. Thus wo-men's vulnerability to being infected and affected by HIV and AIDS is inextricably linked to gender inequality at all levels.

Although some attention is paid to women specific needs in the National HIV and AIDS Policy, there is clearly a need for a comprehensive gender analysis of the policy. Key areas of concern for women include the prevention of parent to child transmission, the provision of anti-retroviral drugs in the public sector and legislation regarding post exposure prophylaxis.

With more than four million adults infected with HIV, and growing numbers of AIDS related deaths, South Africa still has one of the biggest and most rampant HIV epidemics in the world. This has profound social and economic effects, and impacts particularly severely on women. Department of Health prevalence surveys among pregnant women attending state funded antenatal clinics estimated that 27.9 percent of pregnant women were living with HIV in 2003. As demonstrated in Table 22, HIV infection continues to rise amongst all age groups.

Of the 5.6 million South Africans who were HIV positive at the end of 2003, 55 percent were female and 96,228 were babies. In producing these figures, it is assumed that pregnant women accurately represented all women aged 15-49 years, that men were 85 percent as likely to be infected as women, and that 30 percent of babies born to infected mothers would themselves be HIV-positive (ignoring any reductions due to preventative action). According to these figures, around 22.8 percent of all South Africans over 15 years old were HIV-positive in 2003.

As the Table 22 reveals, among females, prevalence is highest in those between 25 and 29 years old; among males, the peak is in the group aged 30-34 years.

The South African Human Development Report (1998) noted with concern the increasing number of women in monogamous relationships in rural areas, who became infected with HIV because of their sole partner's risky behaviour. In addition, high levels of violence in South Africa render women more vulnerable. A 2003 research suggested that domestic violence and women's

Estimated HIV Prevalence among South Africans by Age, 2003		Table 22
Age (years)	Male prevalence %	Female prevalence %
2-14	5	6
15-19	4	7
20-24	8	17
25-29	22	32
30-34	24	24
35-39	18	14
40-44	12	19
45-49	12	11
50-55	5	8
55+	7	7
Total	9.5	12.8

SOURCE South African Department of Health Study, 2003.

perceptions of their degree of control in their relationships (which are indicative of unequal power relations) are important predictors of HIV and are associated with increased risk of HIV infection.[107]

Poverty and economic inequality make women dependent on men, more vulnerable to domestic violence and less able to negotiate safer sex practices. The need to supplement income may force women to sell sex either as sex workers or in a less formal sex-for-support relationship. Poverty not only shapes vulnerability to infection, it also impacts on access to healthcare and household status. Poor women are less able to access healthcare services to protect themselves against infection (e.g. by getting treatment for sexually transmitted diseases) or to care for themselves and their families. For many working class families, AIDS brings an added social and economic burden. Ill health means increased expenses on healthcare, and death brings additional burial costs. The constant threat that the current breadwinner and/or future breadwinner may die means a loss of income for the family.

For many it also means a loss of housing and medical benefits for the remaining members. The constant stereotyping of women as caretakers implies a reduction in employment opportunities. Many women give up their jobs to look after infected family members. For many women, being infected with HIV or living in a family that is affected by HIV means that their lives enter a downward spiral from which there is little escape.

Vertical transmission is exacerbated by poverty. Breastfeeding carries a substantial risk of HIV transmission. Women with HIV and who are unemployed are often unable to afford milk formula. McCoy (2002) adds that traditional socio-cultural norms and perceptions also contribute to the continuous practice of breastfeeding. Poverty also means the lack of access to clean water and electricity that are necessary to prevent other infections in a newborn infant.

Because HIV and AIDS have multiple causes, it requires a multi-sectoral response. Healthcare is central to this, but government, as a whole needs to address AIDS. Thus The Abuja Declaration expects governments to recognise the particular vulnerability of women, especially the impact of "economic and social inequalities and traditionally accepted gender roles that leave them in a subordinate position to men" (paragraph seven). It commits government to political leadership and commitment at the highest level and to mainstreaming by ensuring a gender perspective in all national policy-making and programme implementation relating to HIV and AIDS (paragraph 24). It also calls for a co-ordinated multi-sectoral response with a gender perspective in all national policy-making and programme implementation (paragraph 24).

HIV, AIDS and healthcare
The National AIDS Plan and various updates locate HIV and AIDS health services within the primary healthcare system. Policies on prevention include:
- promotion of safer sex practices (although not gendered);
- promotion of improved health-seeking behaviour (although not gendered);
- improving access to male and female condoms; and
- reducing mother to child transmission by

Estimated HIV Prevalence among Antenatal Clinic Attendees by Age, 2001-2003				Table 23
Age group (years)	2000 prevalence %	2003 prevalence %	2001 prevalence %	2002 prevalence %
20	16.1	15.4	14.8	15.8
20-24	29.1	28.4	29.1	30.3
25-29	30.6	31.4	34.5	35.4
30-34	23.3	25.6	29.5	30.9
35-39	15.8	19.3	19.8	23.4
40+	11.0	9.8	17.2	15.8

SOURCE: South African Department of Health Study, 2003.

○ improving access to voluntary counselling and testing (VCT),

○ family planning,

○ developing clinical guidelines for reducing transmission at child-birth, and

○ rolling out a package of service including anti-retroviral therapy to HIV positive pregnant women.

The Plan committed to investigate options for appropriate post-exposure services for victims of sexual abuse.

Anti-retrovirals (ARVs) to prevent vertical transmission are available in public hospitals, as is ARV treatment for people living with AIDS. In both instances, the implementation has been slow. In the former instance, AIDS activists went to court to speed up delivery.[108] The roll-out of ARVS has been plagued by political controversies, as well as infrastructural problems such as staff shortages and inadequate drug supply. By August 2005, the majority of the 70,000 people receiving ARVs from state hospitals were women, and about 10 percent were children.[109] Since 2002, Post Exposure Prophylaxis (PEP) for victims of sexual assault has been available in the public sector.

Social welfare

The AIDS Plan addressed the need to deal with caregivers and Cabinet committed to assisting families affected by the AIDS epidemic and to improving the system of home-based and community-based care. The Department of Social Development (DSD) has identified the mitigation of the social and economic effects of HIV and AIDS on vulnerable gro-ups as a priority area and has developed policy on this. How-ever, there appears to be no gender analysis in this policy. The overall emphasis is on children.[110]

The DSD is also responsible for the provision of economic reso-urces, which are mainly targeted at women as caregivers (child support grant) and on old people (pension). Disability grants can be accessed by people living with AIDS where their CD count drops below 200, for a renewable period of one year. There is some evidence that these grants allow people living with AIDS to improve nutrition and health. However, the need to renew annually and the nature of the test means that people lose the grant as their health improves often forcing them into choices between health and the grant.[111]

Stigma and discrimination

The Plan also addresses the need to deal with stigma and discrimination – although not specifically in relation to women. Research on this shows that stigma is gendered and deeply embedded in society.[112]

Women's vulnerability to HIV and AIDS in South Africa is shaped by social and cultural norms. In some instances, the resurgence and/or reinvention of traditional and conservative norms of gender and sexuality is viewed as a form of dealing with the epidemic, of placing blame on women (or young women) and as seeking ways to stem infections. The emergence of virginity testing in Kwazulu-Natal is partly explained by this.[113]

Sexually Transmitted Infections[114]

In South Africa, it is estimated that 11 million sexually transmitted infection (STIs) cases occur annually. Epidemiological and biological factors provided evidence that STIs are considered co-factors in the transmission of HIV and AIDS. Controlling STIs has therefore become a high priority for the South African government and is a main strategy for HIV control.

Addressing the impact   Box 6
of HIV and AIDS on
women and children

The Joint Monitoring Committee on the Improvement of Quality of Life and Status of Women tabled a report titled "How Best can South Africa Address the Horrific Impact of HIV and AIDS on Women and Children" in parliament in 2001. In its report, it noted that rich and middle class South Africans who were HIV-positive or had AIDS could choose to access Anti-Retroviral treatment. They had access to adequate nutrition and could choose to follow a healthy lifestyle. In contrast, however, poor people had no such options. Too often they have limited access to the basics such as water, nutrition, and good healthcare including treatment. The report recommended that Anti-Retrovirals be given to raped women as post-exposure prophylaxis for rape.

Source South Africa Survey 2001/02

Access to medical aid

In South Africa, medical aid schemes are quite efficient in providing for specialised, long-term healthcare. Yet, among the many forms of healthcare, medical aid schemes have been the most non-egalitarian. Thus, the unemployed, those in lower-income brackets and numerous South African women employed in the informal sector, (domestic workers or contract workers) rarely benefit from medical aid schemes. According to the October 1995 Household Survey, only 23 percent men of 18 years and more and 20 percent women had access to medical aid. In all the population groups, women had less access to medical aid. Access to this facility is also racially biased.

According to 2001 Statistics, South African Whites made up 44 percent of those with medical aid coverage, followed by Blacks (40 percent), Coloured (11 percent) and Indians (five percent). It remains a fact that the poor and destitute have no access to private and advanced medical care. This situation greatly impacts on women's ability to seek medical help. Overall, statistics SA reports that 58.55 percent women who were medically sick in 2002 did not seek medical help. Amongst these, 25.48 percent cited high medical costs as the reason for not seeking help, whilst 8.53 percent cited that medical help was too far away from where they lived.

VIOLENCE AGAINST WOMEN

The struggle to ensure the safety of women in society remains an ongoing challenge. While progress has been recorded in achieving the Beijing objective of integrated measures to prevent and eliminate violence against women, gender-based violence continues to place women at risk in South Africa.

Violence against women manifests itself in different forms. Violence is both a cause and a consequence of the disempowerment of women in decision-making.[115] Research findings indicate that 25 percent of women in South Africa have experienced physical violence from an intimate partner. In addition to injury, disability, and death, gender-based violence is also associated with physical and mental health problems including HIV, STIs, depression, anxiety disorders, substance use, chronic pain, miscarriage, teenage pregnancy and ante-partum haemorrhage.

Rape

In the year 2000, 52,550 cases of rape and attempted rape of women were reported to the South African police, 21,438 of which were minors under the age of 18 years and of these 7,898 were under the age of 12 years (mostly between seven and 11 years). The highest risk group for sexual assault are teenagers and young women. Child rape accounted for a staggering 40 percent of the rapes reported in 2000. Marital rape remains seriously unreported.

Organisations dealing with gender-based violence have reported that it is never an easy decision for many women to report their husbands, as they fear retaliation.

The South African Police Service (SAPS) estimates that only one in five rape cases are reported to them. It is estimated that only one out of 20 rape cases are reported. Reasons for under-reporting of rape include:
+ Prevailing gender inequality and the fact that the responsibility for curbing sexual desire has been made a woman's responsibility;
+ The poor proximity of police stations and hospitals;
+ Prohibitive transport costs;
+ Lack of adequate ambulance services;

Gender-based violence and HIV converge in a number of ways.

◆ Lack of knowledge of their rights on the part of women;
◆ The secondary victimisation by service providers;
◆ Lack of confidence in the criminal justice system as a rape case can take up to 18 months to be finalised; and
◆ Few convictions. Convictions were only achieved in eight percent of the cases reported in 2000, and conviction rates have declined by four percent between 1999 and 2000.[116]

Femicide

Femicide is defined as the killing or murder of women by their husbands or partners, because they are women. The statistics on femicide in South Africa remained stable for the period 1990-1999. Research by Vetten in 2003 indicates that the profile of the perpetrator is usually men in their late 20s and early 30s. The profile of the victim is often women in their early-30s. In 68 percent of cases, there are witnesses and in 14 percent, the witnesses are the couple's children.[117]

However, in 14 percent of the cases, the men commit suicide afterwards and in three percent of the cases, they unsuccessfully attempt suicide. In 10 percent of the cases, they kill or injure others, such as the women's family or the couple's children. In at least two percent of cases, the women were pregnant at their time of death. In one percent of the cases, the men employed a third party to kill the women. In the majority of the cases, women died a brutal death, with 53 percent of them sustaining injuries all over their bodies. Some women, might have lived, the study found, if the criminal justice system handled the complaints correctly.

Domestic violence

The extent of domestic violence can be extrapolated from community-based, local and regional studies. Estimates range from one in two to one in six women experiencing domestic violence.[118] Many South African women experience domestic violence as a lived reality, and in ways that are both global and uniquely South African. There is consensus that the extent of domestic violence in a particular society is shaped by the relative strength of patriarchy within that society.[119] In South Africa, the intersection between patriarchy and the legacy of racist domination has resulted in particular characteristics to the phenomenon of domestic violence.

Coercive sex

Linked to both sexual assault and domestic violence are the reported high levels of coercive sex in relationships in South Africa. The results of a National Youth Survey were:
◆ 39 percent of sexually experienced girls had been forced to have sex when they did not want to;
◆ 35 percent of sexually experienced boys agree with the statement that "having many partners means I am cool or hip";
◆ 16 percent of sexually experienced girls have had sex in exchange for money, drinks, food or other gifts.[120]

Gender violence, HIV and AIDS

Vetten and Bhana suggest that gender-based violence and HIV converge in a number of ways.[121] Most obviously, rape directly increases women's risk of HIV infection. However, abusive relationships generally constrain women's ability to negotiate safer sex. Recent research has suggested that domestic violence and women's perceptions of their degree of control in their relationships (which are indicative of unequal power relations) are important predictors of HIV and are associated with increased risk of HIV infection.[122]

MEDIA
Portrayal of women

In contemporary South Africa, the mass media is a crucial instrument of communication reproducing social images, and, in particular, reproducing gender stereotypes and messages.

Vast discrepancies exist between women and men in the South African media, with women being under-represented in terms of both their appearance in media content as well as their appointment to positions of power in media organisations.

The South African media displays familiar problems in their portrayal of women. Sexism is evident in the construction of women in print, broadcast and online media. Through news worthiness and other criteria by which material is selected, and in the presentation of content, the media marginalise women and produce negative and stereotyped depictions, which belittle women's contributions to society. News and entertainment media cast women in a narrow range of roles, which treat them as sex objects and define them in terms of their relationship to men. As a result, women are depicted predominantly as entertainers or as victims.

Research confirms these sexist practices. According to a 1995 study, women constituted only 18 percent of the people who appeared in the media, while men constituted 82 percent.[123]

A three-day survey conducted in 1999 to investigate the coverage of women on a daily basis across a variety of South African media indicated that what the media conveyed is a view of predominantly young, White women in entertainment roles.[124] The researchers note that the preponderance of women in "passive and limiting roles" in which they provide pleasure for men or serve as entertainers obscures women's efforts in society.[125]

Meanwhile, the 1995 data confirmed that women tend to be depicted in the media either as victims or in positions of high authority.[126] Research on women politicians shows that women in powerful positions were subjected to severe criticism in the media, which is not applied to their male counterparts.[127]

Women as sources of news

A related concern is the disproportional use of women as sources for news. Not only do male reporters outnumber women in the South African media, but the media also cites predominantly male newsmakers as "experts" in news reports.[128] This practice lends credibility and importance to men's opinions, while women's views remain unheard, unless articulated by men. An important survey of news media in the region commissioned by Gender Links and the Media Institute of Southern Africa (MISA) in 2002 reports that women account for only 19 percent of known news sources in South Africa. However, the situation varies between media, with the use of women as sources ranging between 29 percent and eight percent across the 25 print and broadcast media sampled. According to the same research, Black women as sources are particularly lacking; constituting only five percent of news sources.[129]

Women's voices

Of concern is also the absence of women's voices in particular topics in the media. The media's treatment of women in politics has attracted particular attention.

Women constitute more than 30 percent of representation in government at national level, 28 percent at provincial level and 28 percent at local level, yet research conducted on the 1999 and 2004 general elections in South Africa indicates a "very worrying" absence of women as sources of information in election-related news.[130] In 1999, women constituted eight percent of the gender-specified sources used in election news and information, while 87 percent of news sources were male.

The 1999 report relates the low visibility of women in media coverage to the fact that the media favour socially powerful people and tend to quote senior sources.[131] Meanwhile, the focus on personalities rather than issues adversely affects the treatment of gender topics in the election coverage. In the 2004 national elections, the use of women as sources of news increased to an average of 22 percent.[132] This was partly a result of 10 percent more women being elected to Parliament.[133]

The omission of women's viewpoints and neglect of issues of concern to women, which can be expected to accompany male domination of media, is evident. Studies show that media coverage of women's issues centre on the few topics of crime, violence against women and gender equality.[134] Women in politics and topics affecting women are neglected in political coverage.[135]

A study conducted in 1996 and 1997 on South Africa's new abortion legislation revealed that coverage of the subject was fairly extensive, but was polarised and failed to adopt a woman's perspective or to address the issue in terms of the potential empowerment of women through choice.[136]

A draft editorial policy for the public broadcaster, the South African Broadcasting Service (SABC), was debated in 2003, with input from civil society organisations. Discussions raised the issue of relevance of the media to women, focusing on the neglect of women's viewpoints and gender issues, violent content and the need to protect children from unsuitable material and stereotyping. The Independent Broadcast-

ing Authority (IBA) (now the Independent Communications Authority of South Africa (ICASA)), advocated for the prohibition of material which promotes violence, and recommended particular clauses, which limit the depiction of violence against women in the media.

Women in the media industry

The recommendations on media made by the Fourth United Nations Conference on Women in Beijing in 1995 show how necessary it is for women to occupy decision-making positions in media structures, to encourage change and to have access to communication technology to disseminate their views.[137]

Surveys conducted in 2002 reported the continuing under-representation of women in the media profession in South Africa.[138] According to a national skills audit commissioned by the South African National Editors' Forum (SANEF), newsrooms still display a gender imbalance. Contrastingly, however, women predominate in reporting and management positions in certain sections of news organisations.[139]

The 2002 research by Gender Links and MISA noted that while women often serve as presenters in broadcasting, the presence of women in the print industry is only 29 percent.[140] This study also reports a racial dimension to the situation. In particular, the report emphasised the lack of young, Black women in the media, who accounted for only six percent of media professionals.[141]

Meanwhile, the SANEF skills audit recorded a perception that women are more suitable for covering "softer" news.[142]

A pressing concern is the lack of women who feature in top editorial, decision-making, and managerial positions in the media. This is despite slight improvements reported on the situation towards

2000. There is especially a dearth of either Black or White women editors in the newspaper industry in South Africa. If women do not occupy such positions, the interests of women cannot be articulated.

The situation of women in the media was raised at the Human Rights Commission's hearings into racism in the media in 2000. The commission heard of particular problems which are experienced by Black women in the media industry, and that the low number of Black women journalists, in particular, needs to be addressed.[143]

Women's voices may have better opportunity of being heard outside of the mainstream media.[144]

There is little doubt that internet communications technology and woman-centred websites are assisting women throughout Africa to obtain information and to network.[145] However, gender dimensions of such media have not been thoroughly investigated and women's access and use could still be limited.[146] Moreover, the warning has been issued from the outset that such media may repeat situations where women have been denied access to media through lack of appropriate skills and training.[147]

The question is not only about information provision and networking, but whether the new media can provide for more women's views to be aired, and in their own voice.

INFORMATION COMMUNICATION TECHNOLOGIES

The challenge for government on this sector has been to gear ICTs towards development goals, and using ICTs to ensure that basic needs, including health provision, education and social grants are accessible. An important innovation has been ensuring that the content is appropriate for the needs of the poor, especially women, and that sufficient attention is given to the needs of women entrepreneurs.

ENVIRONMENT

The situation as it relates to women's interaction with the environment has not changed dramatically since the last report was written. Women in both urban and rural areas are responsible for managing the household and ensuring that day-to-day needs are met in terms of water, energy and food. Deterioration in land and water resources greatly hinders women's ability to carry out both productive and reproductive roles.

Though there has been some policy and programme developments in South Africa, women particularly rural women, continue to be absent from structures and processes which involve decisions with regards to the management of environmental resources. What is also lacking is a gender analysis in discussions around environment, thereby pointing to research gaps and capacities in gender analysis in discussions on environment in the region. In addition, the majority of women in South Africa, particularly Black women in rural areas, generally lack access and control of natural resources such as land, water and energy resources and have high poverty levels.

Millennium Development Goals Box 7

There are eight Millennium Development Goals (MDGs). For each goal one or more targets have been set, most for 2015, using 1990 as a benchmark.

♦ **Eradicate extreme poverty and hunger**
Targets 2015 Halve the proportion of people whose income is less than one dollar a day, and halve the proportion of people who suffer from hunger.

♦ **Achieve universal primary education**
Target 2015 Ensure that all girls and boys will be able to complete primary school.

♦ **Promote gender equality and empower women**
Targets 2005, 2015 Eliminate gender disparity in primary and secondary education preferably by 2005 and at all levels of education no later than 2015.

♦ **Reduce child mortality**
Target 2015 Reduce by two-thirds the mortality rate of children under five.

♦ **Improve maternal health**
Target 2015 Reduce by three-quarters the ratio of women dying in childbirth.

♦ **Combat HIV and AIDS, malaria and other diseases**
Target 2015 Halt and begin to reverse the spread of HIV and AIDS, and the incidence of malaria and other major diseases.

♦ **Ensure environmental sustainability**
Integrate the principles of sustainable development into country policies and programmes and reverse the loss of environmental resources.
Target 2015 Reduce by half the proportion of people without access to safe drinking water.
Target 2020 Achieve significant improvement in the lives of at least 100 million slum dwellers.

♦ **Develop a global partnership for development**
Develop an open, rule-based, predictable, non-discriminatory trading and financial system that include a commitment to good governance, development and poverty reduction – nationally and internationally.
Address the special needs of the least developed countries, and landlocked and small Island developing states.
Deal comprehensively with the debt problems of developing countries.
Develop decent and productive work for youth.
In cooperation with pharmaceutical companies, provide access to affordable essential drugs in developing countries.
In cooperation with the private sector, make available the benefits of new technologies – especially information and communications technologies.

SOURCE www.undp.org

PART II
POLICIES AND PROGRAMMES

This section outlines the policies and programmes that the government has put in place to achieve gender equality in South Africa. The section also highlights what developments have occurred in policies and programmes to address gender inequalities since the last profile was written and obstacles and achievements towards advancement of women in different sectors. These are assessed in relation to South Africa's international commitments, especially as identified in CEDAW and the Millennium Development Goals.

The achievement of gender equality is a policy priority in South Africa. The commitments and specific priorities guiding this are set out in international, regional and national policy frameworks. This section identifies the frameworks, mechanisms of policy implementation achievements and obstacles to the adva-ncement of women in different sectors.

INTERNATIONAL POLICY FRAMEWORKS

The South African government has ratified or signed most of the international women's rights ins-truments. These include the Convention on the Elimination of All Forms of Discrimination Aga-inst Women (CEDAW) and the Beijing Platform For Action (BPFA). However, South Africa has not yet ratified the Optional Protocol, which was adopted by State Parties to CEDAW in 2002. By ratifying the Optional Proto-col, a State recognises the compe-tence of the Committee on the Elimination of Discrimination ag-ainst Women, the body that mon-itors State parties' compliance with the Convention to receive and consider complaints from individuals or groups within its jurisdiction.

South Africa has also signed the UN's Convention on Trans-national Organised Crime and its two protocols to Prevent, Supp-ress, and Punish Trafficking in Persons, Especially Women and Children. South Africa has also rat-ified important International Labour Organisation conventions: the Convention on Workers with Family Responsibilities; Co-nvention concerning Equal Remu-neration for Men and Women Workers for Work of Equal Value, No. 100; the Convention on Discri-mination No 110 and the Maternity Rights 183.

At regional level, South Africa has signed the African Charter on Human and People's Rights, as well as the Protocol to the African Charter on Human and Peoples' Rights on the Rights of Women in Africa. South Africa is also a mem-ber of the Commonwealth, which has adopted a number of signifi-cant agreements and declarations that seek to promote and protect gender equality.

At the sub-regional level, South Africa, as a member of the Southern African Development Community (SADC) agreed to the SADC Declaration on Gender and Development as well as its Adden-dum on the Prevention and Eradi-cation of Violence Against Women and Children adopted by SADC Heads of State and Government in 1997 and 1998 respectively.

South Africa is obligated to present regular reports to all of the above bodies. As a result of its in-volvement in these bodies and the government's commitment to gen-der equality, government depart-ments have developed gender poli-cies in line with their functions.

For the purposes of this report, two of the most important interna-tional standards have been identi-fied as a basis for measuring

achievements and obstacles to change in respect of gender equality in South Africa. These are CEDAW and the Millennium Development Goals (MDGs). CEDAW is based on the understanding that discrimination against women violates the principles of equality of rights and respect for human dignity. It highlights the need for State parties to introduce measures that combat discrimination against women in all spheres of society. The MDGs, agreed on by world leaders at the Millennium Summit in September 2000, establish an ambitious agenda for reducing poverty and improving lives.

Both of these documents are central to the government's gender mainstreaming policies and programmes. They set obligations and benchmarks to allow for measurement of progress within a particular institution or society.

NATIONAL POLICY FRAMEWORKS[148]

The Constitution of the Republic of South Africa, 108 of 1996, is the supreme law in South Africa, which sets the standards for all government action. It demonstrates a strong commitment to gender equality, which is a foundational value of South Africa's democracy,[149] and sets rigorous standards to the advancements of women's human rights. Thus, it has a strong and substantive equality protection[150] and detailed rights for women which include rights to freedom and security of the person that are explicit on bodily autonomy, freedom from violence and reproductive choice[151] and a prohibition against any expression that amounts to advocating gender hatred and constitutes incitement to harm.[152]

The Constitution also entrenches socio-economic rights.[153] Importantly, the Constitution makes cultural and religious laws and practices subject to the constitution, and thus to the equality right. The

Constitutional Court has read this to mean that customary law, for example, must be free from gender discrimination. Finally, the Constitution established an independent constitutional body to promote gender equality – the Commission for Gender Equality.[154]

The Constitution sets the legal and normative framework for national policies. Primary among these for women is the National Policy Framework for Women's Empowerment and Gender Equality,[155] the "Gender Policy Framework" finalised by the Office on the Status of Women (OSW) in 2000. It outlines the principles for government to achieve the mainstreaming of gender equality. It is a guiding framework rather than a specific plan of action, which sets particular goals and targets. The implementation of the broad principles is left to the different national and provincial government structures and departments. The main objectives of the policy with regard to gender mainstreaming are:

+ To establish policies, programmes, structures and mechanisms to empower women and to transform gender relations in all aspects of work, at all levels of government as well as well as within broader society;
+ To ensure that gender considerations are effectively integrated into all aspects of government policies, activities and programmes; and
+ To establish an institutional framework for the advancement of the status of women as well as the achievement of gender equality.

In the same year, the Commission for Gender Equality (CGE) prepared the "Framework for Transforming Gender Relations in South Africa" as a measure to fill the gap created by the absence of a national policy. The framework is based on the need to:
+ Move towards a popular understanding of gender equality;

- Develop an indigenous policy approach to the transformation of gender relations;
- Raise awareness of the constitutional roles and responsibilities of the various role players, including men and women in civil society;
- Highlight the commitments made by government to various regional and international agreements advancing gender equality; and
- Illustrate how women and men can plan, develop and implement programmes for the advancement of gender equality.

These are to be achieved through two mechanisms. Firstly, the CGE aimed to provide"user-friendly" tools for policy-makers and programme planners in government, public and statutory bodies, private businesses, enterprises and institutions. Secondly, it aimed to "canvas the views of the identified target [beneficiaries] in the development, implementation and monitoring of public policy."[156] As an analytical document, it is a good resource but has not been used as a basis for action in the achievement of gender equality. In part this is because the framework and the process of laying out baseline indicators was seen by the OSW as its job; as a result the process was not taken very far.

In addition, there are national policy frameworks within each sector and these vary in their commitment and ability to promote gender equality.

POLICY IMPLEMENTATION
The national framework[157]
Policy implementation in South Africa occurs within an overall framework of integrated governance.

In 1994, the government inherited a state that paid little attention to co-ordinated action, effective planning and careful costing, considered budgetary processes and monitoring and evaluation of its output. The last few years have seen significant changes being introduced to the policy development and implementation cycle. These include integrated governance, introduced in 2001, to accelerate effective service delivery. This involves interactive and integrated governance that seeks to improve co-ordination of efforts to transform the public service and of monitoring and evaluation systems.[158]

The government has created five cluster areas, grouping the 27 different ministries: Social Sector; Justice, Crime Prevention and Security; Economy and Employment; International Relations, Peace and Security; and Governance and Administration. The clusters were envisioned to deal with crosscutting issues, which, in reality, did not happen. A major challenge for government is to integrate gender across these five clusters.

The Medium Term Strategic Framework and Medium Term Expenditure Framework set up a three-year budgetary and planning cycle. Government departments are expected to plan and cost effectively in order to obtain budgetary allocations for their personnel and programmes. They are also expected to align national, provincial and local policy, planning and programme priorities with each other and with the overall policy goals of government. Monitoring and evaluation systems are an integral part of effective governance and delivery. These were virtually absent before 1994 and are in the process of being developed.

In addition, government seeks participation from the public in a variety of formal and informal ways. One of these is the use of *imbizos*; meetings held by the President at provincial level to identify needs. The national priorities are drawn from the *imbizos* outcomes.

Gender policy framework

After 1994, South Africa adopted the idea of gender mainstreaming through the establishment of a National Machinery for Women. This was regarded internationally as "best practice" for ensuring that governments addressed the needs of women. The performance of the South African government in this regard has been seen as particularly important. It is well positioned to act as a role model in respect of gender mainstreaming. The United Nations defines national machinery for women as "a single body or complex organised system of bodies, often under different authorities but recognised by the Government as the institution dealing with promotion of the status of women."[159]

South Africa put in place a "package" of structures to integrate gender into all aspects of policy formulation and implementation. These are:

◆ Government structures. namely, the Office on the Status of Women, based in the Office of the Presidency and Gender Focal Points in national line ministries.[160] These structures are replicated at provincial level.[161]
◆ A parliamentary structure. the Joint Monitoring Committee on the Improvement of the Quality of Life and Status of Women.[162]
◆ Commission for Gender Equality. a national, independent monitoring body, which is directly accountable to Parliament.[163]

The provincial structures are made up of the Provincial OSW and the gender focal points in the provincial government departments.

Office on the Status of Women

The Office on the Status of Women (OSW) was established in 1997. It is currently in the President's office and reports to a Deputy Minister. The head of the OSW is a civil servant. Its roles include:

◆ Developing and implementing a National Policy on Gender;
◆ Supporting government departments and public bodies to mainstream gender in all policies and programmes and promoting affirmative action within government;
◆ Organising gender training for government departments;
◆ Initiating cross-departmental initiatives; and
◆ Monitoring and evaluating government programmes, in part through the development of indicators.

The OSW is thus the pinnacle of the national machinery as well as the co-ordinating structure for gender mainstreaming. In fulfilling that mandate, it has been hamstrung by its level of authority and a shortage of resources.

Departmental Gender Focal Points/Gender Equity Units

Each ministry and department is expected to establish a gender unit and put in place a gender policy. However, these structures have not been as effective as envisaged in the design of the machinery.

A study conducted by the OSW based on a questionnaire distributed to 36 departments,[164] found that 24 out of 25 responding departments reported they had Gender Focal Points (GFPs). However, only eight percent of the responding departments had a GFP at the level recommended by the National Policy Framework and the majority of the GFPs and their supervisors are below entry point managerial level. Personnel are often not trained effectively nor do they have capacity to influence policy. This means that they are not in a position to perform the gender mainstreaming functions in their departments. In addition, 84 percent of GFPs reported that they performed functions other than their GFP work. The report concludes that "South Africa is not in a position to report on progress with regard to Strategic Objective H of the BPFA (gender mainstreaming) eight years after signing the document, and despite eight years of democracy."[165]

Local government machineries

There is a gap in the local government structures with regard to gender structures. In an effort to fill this vacuum, the South African Local Government Association (SALGA) established a Gender Working Group that supports women councillors in local government. Although SALGA is responsible for the training of civil officials, gender training is not its priority.

Joint Monitoring Committee

The Joint Committee on the Improvement of the Quality of Life and Status of Women was established in 1996 as an *ad hoc* committee of Parliament. In 1997, it became a joint standing committee with higher status and more powers, mainly concerned with overseeing the implementation of CEDAW and BPFA. It has interpreted this role widely to include consultations with civil society in relation to key legislation and policy areas (such as domestic violence, customary law, termination of pregnancy and HIV and AIDS).

This committee has also been a partner in the internationally groundbreaking work on the Women's Budget Initiative. This initiative seeks to disaggregate and track government spending along gender lines. The Central Statistical Service (CSS) now uses gender disaggregated data in the compilation of its reports and similarly, the Department of Finance used a gender analysis in its 1998 National Budget Review.

The Committee has functioned fairly effectively in canvassing public response on key policy issues and in calling government departments and minis-

ters to account, even on contentious issues such as HIV and AIDS. It also supported the fast tracking of legislation related to women in the first parliament.

Commission for Gender Equality

The Commission for Gender Equality (CGE) was established in 1996 and is mandated by the South African Constitution as a mechanism for strengthening constitutional democracy. The CGE is mainly responsible for monitoring, evaluation and upholding the constitutional principle of gender equality in public and private domains. The roles and functions of the Commission are wide-ranging. They include:

- Monitoring and evaluating the policies and practices of both government and private sector institutions;
- Public education and information;
- Making recommendations to government to promote gender equality, including recommending changes to existing legislation and proposing new legislation;
- Resolving gender-related disputes through mediation and conciliation or litigation; and
- Investigating gender inequality.

The CGE has been encouraged to play a stronger watchdog role in respect of gender equality.

Challenges on mainstreaming gender

Overall, the national machinery acts as a vehicle through which South Africa can meet its constitutional and international commitments to gender equality, human rights and social justice.[166] In doing this, it has to align itself with the national policy implementation framework described above. This has proved to be a huge challenge and strategies for doing this are still being developed within the Office on the Status of Women (OSW).[167]

Gender Audit findings   Box 8
2003[169]

Of the total 29 departments that responded in 2003, nine (31.03 percent) had Gender Focal Points (GFPs) appointed at the level mandated by the Gender Policy Framework for Women's Empowerment and Gender Equality.

This indicates that less than one-third (31.03 percent) of the National Departments comply with the South African National Policy Framework for Women's Empowerment and Gender Equality of December 2000, and the Cabinet Memorandum of 1996 (No. 3 of 1996, dated 27 June 1996, file number 113/1/1/1).

Out of the 29 responding departments in 2003, the GFPs were structured as follows:

+ For 16 departments, the term GFP refers to an individual.
+ For 13 departments, the term GFP refers to a unit.
+ Nine departments reported that they have GFPs at the Director level.
+ Eleven reported their GFPs were at Deputy Director level.
+ Six reported that their GFPs were Assistant Directors.
+ Fifteen departments had formally appointed GFPs, i.e. the person's performance contract referred to their function as that of a GFP.
+ Eleven departments assess the GFPs for what can be referred to as gender management work.[clxx]
+ Six departments have three people or less in the unit.
+ Two departments have more than five persons in the gender unit.[170]
+ Sixteen of the responding departments indicated that GFPs reported directly or indirectly to a supervisor with gender as a key performance area.
+ Ten of the responding departments did not provide an answer to this question or were unsure of the status in this regard.
+ In three departments GFPs perform three functions or less.
+ Fourteen of the responding departments carry out four or more functions over and above the gender tasks.

Critically, this will depend on the ability of gender experts across government to intervene in the planning process and then to monitor progress. At present, this does not seem to be occurring enough and gender often seems to be outside of the "mainstream" policy and planning process – largely because of problems of capacity, authority and resources as discussed above.

The OSW is in the process of defining entry points to this core policy process. These might include:

+ The identification and inclusion of gender indicators;
+ Providing for gender to be an integral part of the cluster reports to cabinet; and
+ Requiring departments to provide an explanation of how a particular policy or programme impacts on gender when it is being discussed in cabinet.[168]

The challenge is both to address some of the shortcomings of the National Machinery and to build its capacity to mainstream gender into the general policy framework across the three levels of government – national, provincial and local. To assist this, the OSW, located in the President's Office, can access the Policy Unit in the same office, which is tasked with providing government with policy direction as well as strategy on vision for the future.

It is also critical that the Gender Focal Points are able to access the decision-making nexus within the government departments. As mentioned above, problems of capacity, authority and resources mean that this is extremely difficult and gender issues tend not to reach decision-making structures within departments. The presidency has now introduced a directorate for programmes to interface with the Chief Directorates' cluster, in an effort to facilitate gender mainstreaming in the cluster ministries.

There is a need for greater co-ordination and co-operation between the different departments within government, especially when these departments are tasked with implementing similar policies. At this stage, this seems to be lacking and as such leads to the stagnation of processes.

The critical challenge remains for government national machinery to insert gender at all points of the policy development, implementation and monitoring phases. While considerable effort has been made in South Africa to formulate legislation and policies to promote gender equality, these are often in the "women's sector." Concerted attention needs to be paid to the integration of gender across all policies and to their implementation and monitoring phases in the next period.

As part of its monitoring function, the OSW conducts annual audits to assess compliance by National Departments to the provisions of the National Policy Framework and Strategic Objective H of the BDPFA.

As stated, the audits conducted limited themselves to a narrow and technical reading of the provisions of the Policy Framework; and Cabinet Memorandum No. 3 of 1996, to assess government's compliance with Strategic Objective H of the Beijing Platform for Action. That is, they did not assess skill levels of Gender Managers, and the financial resources allocated for gender within individual departments.

A more thorough analysis of the human resource needs of the gender machinery would indicate that the provisions of the Cabinet Memorandum No. 3 of 1996, as well as the National Policy Framework for Women's Empowerment and Gender Equality do not go far enough to provide South Africa with an effective Gender Machinery. Such an analysis could not be conducted in the earlier phase of governance. Currently, sufficient experience has been gained to allow for a more realistic assessment of what is needed to ensure effective gender mainstreaming.[172]

A key criticism of the gender machinery within government in South Africa is that although there is expressed political will for gender equality, and the responsibility for gender mainstreaming is said to be that of all government officials, accountability for gender mainstreaming resides nowhere within the administration.

HUMAN RIGHTS OF WOMEN

Since 1994 the government has made tremendous strides in ensuring that legislation conforms with the Constitution and international instruments ratified, in particular the Convention on the Elimination of all Forms of Discrimination Against Women, the Convention on the Rights of the Child, the African Charter on Human and Peoples' Rights, and the African Charter on the Rights and Welfare of the Child.

The primary challenge for government, however, is to reduce and eventually eliminate the gap between ambitious legislative measures and actual delivery on the ground. In the face of increasing competition between sectors for scarce resources, the establishment of sustainable plans for the development of vulnerable groups (especially women, children and the elderly) is critical. Monitoring these plans for actual delivery, measured against realistic performance criteria is also essential.

The legislation that has been passed to promote and protect the rights of women must be seen within the context of an integrated government policy that spends an increasing portion of its budget on education and other social sector services. The eradication of poverty is a primary first step to the total

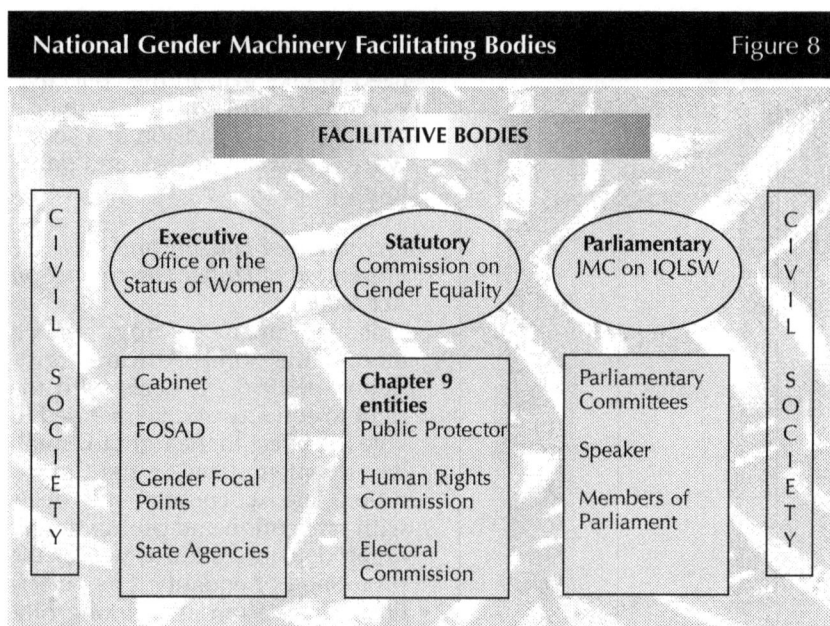

National Gender Machinery Facilitating Bodies — Figure 8

FACILITATIVE BODIES

CIVIL SOCIETY

Executive
Office on the Status of Women

Statutory
Commission on Gender Equality

Parliamentary
JMC on IQLSW

Cabinet

FOSAD

Gender Focal Points

State Agencies

Chapter 9 entities
Public Protector

Human Rights Commission

Electoral Commission

Parliamentary Committees

Speaker

Members of Parliament

CIVIL SOCIETY

eradication of discrimination. The government is aware of how poverty, racism and sexism conspire to place women, especially rural Black women at the very bottom of the human rights hierarchy. The inter-sectionality of race, class and gender demand a holistic approach to women's development that presuppose the provision of dedicated resourcing and the establishment of a targeted and affirming development architecture that is couched in a human rights ethos that recognises that women's rights are human rights.

Despite the enabling and empowering legislation that has been passed since 1994, women continue to face marginalisation and discrimination in their homes, communities and workplaces, bringing into focus that equality is not realised solely through legislation. Equality is a value that needs to be shared and upheld by the entire community – men and women alike. Institutions, too, need to internalise this value and make their environments affirming to all those that enter them. It's a paradigm shift – a mental gear change – that is required. The values of equality, respect and dignity need to take grip in the collective psyche, if South Africa is to realise its Constitution's vision of a society free of racism, sexism and patrimony.

Promotion of Equality and Prevention of Unfair Discrimination Act (2000)

This Act emanates from section nine of the South African Constitution of 1996. It deals with the right to equality and is intended to give full effect to the right to equality as contemplated in the Constitution. The Act consequently deals with prevention and prohibition of unfair discrimination as well as the promotion of equality. The objects of the legislation are, among others, to:

◆ Prevent and prohibit unfair discrimination and to provide redress in cases of unfair discrimination;
◆ Facilitate South Africa's compliance with international human rights treaty obligations, with specific reference to the CEDAW;
◆ Provide for the eradication of current systemic discrimination which is a legacy of previously legalised discrimination;
◆ Provide for the promotion of equality, prioritising the adoption of measures to advance persons disadvantaged by unfair discrimination; and
◆ Provide for measures aimed at ensuring the eradication of unfair discrimination, hate speech and harassment with special focus on race, gender and disability.

Maintenance Act

One of the most critical areas impacting on the basic human rights of women is that of maintenance payment. Multitudes of South African women are wholly or partially dependent on maintenance payment for the livelihood and survival of their children. Defaulting maintenance payers are the cause of untold misery and degradation to children in South Africa. Defaulters who have the means to pay and choose instead to ignore their responsibilities as parents are steadily being brought to book.

The Maintenance Act, enacted in 1998, is intended to bring about a number of improvements in the maintenance system. For example, the appointment of maintenance investigators to track down defaulting parent/s where previously the onus was on the single parent or care-giver to establish the whereabouts of the defaulter; the setting out of core statutory guidelines relating to the duty of support of parents in respect of their children; enabling maintenance courts to make maintenance orders in the absence of the respondent in appropriate cases; and by extending the circumstances in which a maintenance court can order the payment of maintenance to be made on behalf of respondents.

Marriage

Prior to 1994, customary marriages were not recognised. However, now the Recognition of Customary Marriages Act, (No. 120 of 1998), makes provision for the recognition of customary marriages in accordance with customary law or traditional rites. This Act improves the position of women and children within these marriages by introducing measures that bring customary law in line with the Constitution and South Africa's international obligations.

The Act removes elements of discrimination against the customary legal tradition and thereby gives expression to two constitutional principles; namely the rights to systems of family law based on any tradition or religion and the right to cultural pluralism.

Customary Law

Among the most important rec-ommendations of the South African Law Commission, with regard to the reform of the custom-ary law of succession, is the amend-ment of the Intestate Succession Act of 1987. It recommended that the customary law of succession rule of primogeniture be abolished as it discriminates against women. The proposed draft Bill provides that upon a person's death, the estate has to dissolve in accordance with that person's will or where there is no will, according to the law of intestate prescribed by the Intestate Succession Act.

This would apply to all intes-tate estates including the estates of persons who had contracted a cus-tomary marriage, which subsisted at the time of death. In terms of these recommendations, the sur-viving spouse will be entitled to inherit the deceased's house and personal belongings. Where the deceased owned more than one house, it recommends that the sur-viving spouse inherit one house of such spouse's choice.[173]

Legal framework

Table 24 lists some of the key leg-islations and the most critical leg-islation passed since 1995, which impact on women's lives. Table 25 presents two key examples of legislation passed in 1994 and 1996 which has unintended con-sequences on women's lives.

Whilst there is agreement about the progressive nature of the legislative measures put in place, there are also strong challenges emanating from women activists, NGOs and special interest groups, with regard to the country's track record in implementing such legis-lation and policies. Uneven admin-istration of justice and access to rights are often cited among the key reasons compromising women' progress towards equity and full citizenship. Government has now shifted focus to broaden-

ing access to services within the criminal justice system and the implementation of restorative jus-tice. However, there are as yet no comprehensive studies focusing on the gendered impact of such delivery. Even where clear advances have been made, such

Important Legislation Impacting on Women's Lives	Table 24

Legislation	Summary
Constitution of the Republic of South Africa, Act 108 of 1996	Widely acclaimed as one of the world's most progressive Constitutions, asserts in its founding provisions that the democratic state is founded on the values of human dignity, the achievement of equality and advancement of human rights and freedoms, non-racism and non-sexism. The Constitution contains several provisions that advance gender equality. Amongst these is the Equality Clause in the Bill of Rights.
Maintenance Act 99 of 1998	This allows the court to order an employer to deduct maintenance from the salary of the father. It allows the court to appoint maintenance officers who can trace the whereabouts of the father, serve documents and to gather information on the financial position of both parties.
Domestic Violence Act 116 of 1998	Through this Act, women are afforded greater protection against actual or threatened physical violence, sexual, emotional, verbal, psychological and economic abuse as well as intimidation, harassment, stalking, damage to or destruction of property, or entry into their home without consent.
Recognition of Customary 120 of 1998 Marriages Act	This Act abolishes the minority status of women married under customary law and abolishes the marital power of husbands as guardians.
The Domestic Worker Sectoral Determination	This Sectoral Determination is set by the Minister of Labour to ensure that vulnerable workers are protected. It outlines the basic working conditions and minimum wages for domestic workers and gardeners and also makes provision for annual wage increases for these workers. As of 01 November 2003, such full-time employees are to receive a minimum of eight percent increase in wages earned.
Unemployment Insurance Contributions Act 4 of 2002	This Act applies to domestic and seasonal workers and their employers and provides for a monthly contribution of one percent of salary paid to as well as earned by employees and employers to the Unemployment Insurance Fund; as well as enforces the employer to register the employee.
Promotion of Equality and Prevention of Unfair Discrimination Act 4 of 2000	The objectives of the Act include the prevention and prohibition of unfair discrimination, redress for discrimination, the promotion of equality and progressive eradication of discrimination.
South African Citizenship Act 88 of 1995	Citizenship may not be lost or gained due to marriage, giving effect to obligations under CEDAW.

SOURCE Compiled by the Office on The Status of Women, 2006.

Legislation Having Unintended Consequences from a Gender Perspective	Table 25
Legislation	**Summary**
The Restitution of Land Rights Act 22 of 1994	States that priority should be given to people with the most pressing needs. Restitution may disadvantage women as the Act aims to restore land rights to those who had rights before, most of whom are not women.
Legal Aid Amendment Act 20 of 1996	Enables the Legal Aid Board to provide legal representation at state expense for accused persons in deserving cases. The Act is being reviewed, to ensure that any gender bias in the operation of legal aid, whether direct or indirect, is eliminated. The Legal Aid Board is expanding on the past focus on criminal cases to include civil matters and by identifying new ways of reaching vulnerable groups.

SOURCE Compiled by the Office on The Status of Women, 2006

as the creation of an enabling environment, there still is yet to be a holistic review of key judgements in the South African courts.

Efficacy of legislation

In spite of the progressive legislation, women, activists, NGOs and special interest groups still have to challenge government regarding the proper implementation of legislation and policies. Inadequate implementation is often cited as one of the major reasons retarding women's progress towards equity and full citizenship.

The White Paper, for instance, sets specific targets for all government departments. These targets include achieving at least 50 percent Black representations at management level. It specifically focuses on redressing the under-representation of women. It sets the target for 30 percent of women recruits by 1999 and two percent for people with disabilities. The Employment Equity Act No. 55 of 1998 is one of the legislative imperatives applied to redress this inequity. Available data however, show that senior women managers increased from 1995 to 2000 but decreased again in 2001.

POLITICS AND DECISION-MAKING

The Traditional Leadership and Governance Framework Act 2003 (N0 41 2003) requires that at least 30 percent of members of the National House of Traditional Leaders be women. Provincial legislation provides for mechanisms or procedures to allow a sufficient number of women to be represented in the Provincial House of Traditional Leaders, and be elected as representatives to the National House of Traditional Leaders. The Act also requires that the number of women be representative of the traditional leaders within a district or municipality. The Local Government Municipal Systems Act, 2000 (No 32 of 2000) ensures the development of a culture that promotes participatory governance and creates enabling conditions to achieve this. Municipalities are required to take into account the circumstances of women, people with disabilities and youth in development planning through specific processes.

Since 1994, several NGOs have taken on the role of educating women as active voters, creating access for women to parliament and parliamentary procedures. Political parties have recognised

Best practices from South African Courts   Box 9

The outstanding achievements in South Africa in this regard are, *inter alia*, the various amendments to the Criminal Procedure Act 51 of 1977, the minimum sentences for certain offences (The Criminal Law Amendment Act 105 of 1997), the restrictions with regard to bail provisions, the Sexual Offences and Family Courts, labour law developments, the Employment Equity Act, the Domestic Violence Act and the Maintenance Act.

The Constitutional Court in an important judgement awarded the following decisions that have a gender impact:

1   Socio Economic Rights
Grootboom v Oostenberg Municipality and Others 2000 (3) BCLR 277 (C)

The applicants in this matter were squatters who had been evicted. They sought an order against the respondents compelling them to provide adequate basic temporary shelter or housing, for them and their children pending the applicants obtaining permanent accommodation. In addition, they sought to be provided with adequate and sufficient basic nutrition, shelter, social services and healthcare services. The court held that in terms of Section 28 (the rights of children) of the Constitution of the Republic of South Africa Act 108 of 1996, the applicants' children were entitled to be provided with shelter by the appropriate organ of state. The applicant parents were entitled to be accommodated with their children in such shelter. Further, the relevant organ of state was obliged to provide such shelter until such time as the parents were able to shelter their own children.

2   Intestate Succession *Daniels v Campbell NO and Others 2004 (7) BCLR 735 (CC)*

The Intestate Succession Act 81 of 1987 and the Maintenance of Surviving Spouses Act 27 of 1990 conferred on a surviving spouse rights to claim against the estate of a deceased spouse. The applicant in this matter had been married to the deceased in terms of Muslim rites. The marriage was never solemnised according to the requirements of the Marriage Act 25 of 1961. The applicant sought an order recognising her as the spouse of the deceased in terms of the Intestate Succession Act. The Constitutional Court held that the word "spouse" as used in the Intestate Succession Act included the surviving partner of a monogamous Muslim marriage. Further, the word "survivor" as used in the Maintenance of Surviving Spouse Act included the surviving partner of a monogamous Muslim marriage. The court therefore held that the applicant was a "spouse" and "survivor" as referred to in the respective Acts.

3   The Maintenance Act no 99 of 1998 *S v Visser 2002 (1) SACR 50 (KPA)*

Our courts have been stringent with regard to the imposition of sentences in this regard. The appellant and his wife were divorced and he was ordered to pay maintenance of R2, 500 per month for each of his two adopted children. He was in arrears for the amount of R44, 500. The court sentenced him to 1,440 hours of periodical imprisonment.

4   The Criminal Law Amendment Act 105 of 1997

In terms of Section 51 (1) of Act 105 of 1997, a High Court is obliged, if it has convicted a person of an offence referred to in Part 1 of Schedule 2, to sentence the person to imprisonment for life, unless substantial and compelling circumstances exist. The following crimes pertaining particularly to women are listed in Part 1 of Schedule 2:

◆ For murder, when the death of the victim was caused by the accused in committing or attempting to commit or having or after having committed or attempted to commit the crime of rape.

◆ For rape, when it is committed:
  ○ In circumstances where the victim was raped more than once whether by the accused or by any co-perpetrator or accomplice.
  ○ By more than one person, where such persons acted in the execution or furtherance of a common purpose or conspiracy.
  ○ By a person who has been convicted of two or more offences of rape, but has not yet been sentenced in respect of such convictions.
  ○ By a person knowing that he has the Acquired Immune Deficiency Syndrome (AIDS) or the Human Immunodeficiency Virus (HIV). Rape involving the infliction of grievous bodily harm.

◆ For rape when the victim is:
  ○ A girl under the age of 16 years.
  ○ A physically disabled woman who, due to her physical disability, is rendered particularly vulnerable.
  ○ A mentally ill woman as contemplated in section 1 of the Mental Health Act 18 of 1973. The provisions of the aforementioned legislation are utilised on a daily basis in South Africa's High Courts.

SOURCE Advocate Arveena Persad, Senior State Advocate, Office of the Director of Public Prosecutions (WLD).

the importance of the "women's vote" and conducted specific campaigns for women voters. The holding of mock parliaments for women and the girl-child are all indicators of the gendered nature of the electoral process.[174]

ECONOMY
Employment
South Africa has ratified the Conventions of the International Labour Organisation (ILO) and is obligated by the Constitution to address imbalances in employment. Sub-section 4 of the equality clause in the South African constitution expressly states that national legislation must be enacted to prevent or prohibit unfair discrimination. Important pieces of legislation that have been enacted to create an enabling environment for designated groups (Blacks, women and disabled persons) are:

- The Labour Relations Act[175] which in Schedule seven deals with residual unfair labour practices and prohibits unfair discrimination on the bases listed in the schedule which are the same as those listed in the equality clause of the Constitution;
- The Employment Equity Act, which in Chapter Two, deals with the prohibition of unfair discrimination. This chapter reinforces the equality clause and acts as a tool for the implementation of the equality cla-use in the workplace; and
- The Promotion of Equality and Prevention of Unfair Discrimination is intended, as described in Section two, 'to give effect to the letter and spirit of the Constitution, in particular –
  - the equal enjoyment of all rights and freedoms by every person,
  - the promotion of equality,
  - the values of non-racialism and non-sexism contained in

Section one of the Constitution,
- the prevention of unfair discrimination and protection of human dignity as contemplated in Sections nine and 10 of the Constitution.

Besides the international and national requirements for gender equity within the workplace, there is an additional rationale for affirming women in employment; it makes good business sense and is thus a positive benefit for employers. Investing in and developing of South Africa's people will contribute towards sustainability of businesses and future returns. A workforce that reflects the demographics of the country in terms of gender can improve market share, the understanding of markets, and thus the ability to service all current or prospective clients.[176]

South Africa has also ratified Convention 111 of the International Labour Organisation (ILO), which among other things obligates States to take: "... special measures which are designed to meet the particular requirements of persons, who for reasons such as sex, age, disability, family responsibilities or social or cultural status, are generally recognised to require special provision or assistance."

In placing women's issues at the forefront of policy, some of the government commitments require the private sector to:
- Observe national labour, environment, consumer and health and safety laws, particularly those that affect women;
- Adopt policies and establish mechanisms to grant contracts on a non-discriminatory basis; and
- Recruit women for leadership, decision-making and management, as well as provide training programmes on an equal basis with men.

Trade[177]

One of the key industrial policies is the commitment to fostering sustainable development in areas where poverty and unemployment are highest. The Spatial Development Initiatives (SDI) represent one of the key initiatives to implementing this commitment. The SDIs integrate concerns of women who live in areas most affected by poverty. The aim of the SDIs is to fast-track development.

Since the democratic elections of 1994, there has been a steady policy development, which aims to integrate women into the economy. The Department of Trade and Industry has been one of the drivers in the development of policies and legislation, which they view as the impetus needed for creating an enabling environment for women entrepreneurs. In addition to policy and legislative reform, the department is also in the forefront of initiating women into specific programmes and strategies. The joint venture between the Department of Trade and Industry and the South African Women Entrepreneur's Network (SAWEN) is one such example.

The South African National Treasury is attempting to address specific concerns that affect women and their advancement in the economy, through macro-economic frameworks such as the preferential procurement policy.

The Department of Trade and Industry has developed a number of policies that integrate women in trade and in small and medium enterprises. Special attention is given to historically disadvantaged individuals, ensuring they are given opportunities to grow their enterprises.

In the Black Economic Empowerment strategy, government has tried to integrate the gender component by prescribing targets for Black women to ensure them opportunities. As a result, historically disadvantaged individuals have been enabled to participate in the highest decision-making structures in industry, including board and management levels.

The department has also focused on gender equity and promotion of women-owned enterprises and co-operatives. The National Small Business Act of 2002 provides a voice for small businesses in the revision of the definition of small business. The Act mandates institutions to support small businesses.

Women-owned enterprises are a large component of the small and medium economic enterprises. In its "Technology for Women in Business" (TWIB) programme, the Department of Trade and Industry has also identified the need to support women's advancement through technology.

The Mineral and Petroleum Resources Development Act has far reaching implications for changing patterns of economic resources in South Africa. The imperative is to redress historical imbalances on social inequalities in the control of mining resources in the country. The Act creates an enabling environment for historically disadvantaged groups to enter the mining and petroleum industry and benefit from the nation's mineral wealth. The Department of Minerals and Energy has identified the need for skills development and integration of women in the industry. It seeks to facilitate the implementation of employment equity within the industry. The Department is currently developing a Human Resource Development Strategy for the minerals industry. Its approach integrates a Mines Qualifications Authority, which will formulate a comprehensive skills development strategy that will interface education, experience and related advancement training.

The National Skills Development and Strategy (NSDS) and the government's Human Resource Development Strategy (HRDS) were developed in December 2001. The integration of gender in national skills development framework seeks to address specific challenges and concerns women face in trade, employment and development opportunities. The Department of Labour has, in adopting the National Skills Training Strategy, undertaken to ensure that in complementing this strategy, all sectors will comply with the allocation of 54 percent of resources to women, including the budget.

POVERTY
Poverty alleviation initiatives

Poverty, inequality and underdevelopment remain major obstacles to women's advancement in South Africa. Intervention in the economic system is important to achieve economic empowerment, as markets on their own cannot correct distortions. Issues of poverty and economic underdevelopment cannot be tackled in isolation of key areas such as health, education, gender inequalities in key economic sectors and decision-making positions and access to land and resources. South Africa has a holistic approach to the eradication of poverty.

Social assistance and grants are major components of the programmes to eradicate poverty. However access to education, substantive employment, different grants, land and housing amongst others are also part of the poverty eradication strategy.

Social assistance and welfare services grants have played an increasingly important role over the past 10 years in an effort to redress the immense inequalities in the South African society. Social assistance grants and welfare policies are important for women. Women, who by virtue of the fact that they participate more in the informal sector, and/or that they are the majority among the unemployed, and therefore not contributing to social security, are prime recipients of social assistance.

Social grants

Social grants, formerly allocated on a racial basis, have been equalised and extended to all who are in need and eligible. Beneficiaries have increased from 2.6 million in 1994 to 5.1 million in 2003. The poorest 20 percent of households receive the largest amounts from grants. The full impact will only be realised when all who are eligible are registered.[178]

Government has a two-prong approach with regard to the alleviation of poverty and this takes the form of grants and the public works programme. It has been found that the income grants were more successful in targeting the poorest households than the public works programme.

The social assistance programme constitutes a significant[179] proportion of Government expenditure each year. For instance, the take up rate for the Child Support Grant has increased significantly.[180]

Of concern however, are the low percentages of take up among the girl-child. In the 2001/2002 financial year, the girl-child received only 7.89 percent of Child Grants whilst only 4.73 percent of the recipients of Disability Grants were girl-children.[181]

In terms of scope, women and the girl-child benefit from the following grants:[182]

+ Old age grants;
+ Disability grants;
+ Child support grants;
+ Care dependency grants; and
+ Foster care grants.

Apart from individual grants, women also benefit from grants-in-aid given to NGOs and voluntary sectors. The NGO and voluntary sectors play an important role in the provision of services such as the prevention of violence against women and children, skills development and empowerment programmes for women, planned parenthood, nutrition, health, and HIV and AIDS education and support programmes. These grants are also important in developing preschool and small businesses from home and in the community. The council is responsible for making buildings and land available for these services.

The Child Support Grant is given to a maximum of six children in one family who are under the age of seven. The caregiver can be the mother, father, grandparent, relative, or guardian of the child/children.

The Foster Care Grant is for children, who through a court order, are placed in the care of someone else other than their parents.

The Care Dependency Grant is meant for a parent or foster parent who has to take care of a child, one to 18 years old, who is very sick, disabled or in need of medical attention.

The Child Support, Care Dependency, and the Foster Child Grants are of particular importance to women as they are usually the primary caregivers of children. It is also women who usually care for the aged, sick and disabled who in turn receive most of the budget of welfare grants. Women constitute the greater number of the recipients of the old age pension grant. According to the Department of Welfare, the number of beneficiaries who received social assistance grants during the period 1996/7 was almost three million.

There are, however, problems in accessing these state grants. The primary caregiver can for instance only qualify for child support grants if it can be proved that he/she does not, "without good reason," refuse to accept employment or participate in any development programme. The

final decision is based on the discretion of the administrative official and that opens the way for many abuses and inequities.

The age limit for children has also been problematic. The ceiling has currently been lifted from seven to 14 years. The welfare system has been fraught with ghost-beneficiaries. Some beneficiaries do not understand the process of re-registering once their payment has been stopped for some official reason.

The means test requirements differ for various grants. For instance, a woman's marital status influences her eligibility for the Old Age Pension and the Disability Grant. This distinction differentiates inequitably between a single woman and a married one. The latter qualifies for Old Age Pension with a combined income of R23,064 per annum whilst a single woman only qualifies for pension, if her income does not exceed R12,504.

Qualifying calculations also discriminate against couples living together but not married and same-sex couples. The rural/urban divide also influences the allocation of grants disproportionately. In formal urban settings, primary caregivers qualify for the Child Support Grant with an annual income of below R9,600, compared to rural areas and informal settlements with an income of R13,200. This has a very negative effect on poor rural women.

The Social Relief or Distress Grant is provided for a period of three months to people who are in desperate need under particular circumstances. This relief often comes in the form of food coupons or food parcels rather than cash. This form of assistance is valid for three months and is renewable. The process to qualify for social grant relief assistance is beset by many problems and complications including that:
- The grant application for social assistance takes too long and

the survival of the applicant is threatened. The amount paid as relief is deducted from the grant at a later stage.

♦ People who are too sick to work need to prove by means of a medical aid certificate that they will get better within six months.

♦ A single parent who is in the process of trying to get maintenance from the other parent but is unable to do so must prove that the maintenance procedures are in process.

♦ The partner of a single parent has died and left nothing for the family to live on.

♦ The partner of a parent has been sent to a state institution, such as a prison or a hospital for a period of less than six months. This is only applicable if the person was the only breadwinner in the family. This also applies to people awaiting trial.

♦ People who have experienced a disaster such as their house burning down or being flooded. This does not apply when the whole area has been affected and declared a disaster area.

Old age pensions for poor women are by far the most important because women become eligible for pension at the age of 60 (men at 65). The rate of uptake of this grant is 90 percent among Blacks and Coloureds; 60 percent among Indians and 20 percent among the White community. However, one's marital status determines one's eligibility for this grant. For women in poorer communities, sometimes they become the primary breadwinner.

The dependency on old age pensions has increased over the last few years due to the impact of HIV and AIDS on young people, which has placed responsibility on the older generation to take care of them when they become too sick. This responsibility usually falls on women as the stereotypical caregivers within the household. In many instances, the elderly become open to economic and physical abuse by children and they sometimes end up not affording food, water, rent, electricity, and visits to the clinic or hospital.

Home /Community-based care

Home or community-based care aims to provide comprehensive services, including health and social services, by formal and informal caregivers in the home. It encourages participation by people, responds to the needs of people, encourages traditional community life and strengthens mutual aid opportunities and social responsibility to promote, restore and maintain a person's maximal level of comfort, function and health including care towards a dignified death. Home or community-based care services include:

♦ Early identification of families in need, orphans and vulnerable children;

♦ Addressing the needs of child-headed households;

♦ Linking families and caregivers with poverty-alleviation programmes and services in the community;

♦ Patient care and support-related to HIV, AIDS and other chronic conditions;

♦ Information and education;

♦ Patient and family counselling and support;

♦ Addressing discrimination against stigmatisation, disclosures of chronic diseases; and

♦ Family support including capacity-building, family planning, burials, support for children and social services advice.

National School Nutrition Programme

The National School Nutrition Programme targets schools in poorest regions, especially in rural and farm areas and schools serving learners from informal settlements.

Female service-providers are given priority as it is acknowledged that women have become heads of households in poor families and providers for extended and foster families. Wherever possible, skills-development initiatives are implemented in food-production activities such as food gardens and small bakeries.

Foster care grant[183]

Accessing the Child Care Act is hampered by the fact that to qualify for the Foster Grant, the child must be placed in the care of foster parents through the Children's Court. The court process is lengthy and inappropriate for many families who are content with caring for children who are not their own but require support.

The system is open to abuse,[184] as evidence suggests that many parents, who would otherwise be able to care for their children, are abandoning their children to relatives so that these relatives can access the Child Care Grants.

Problems exist with assessing the Child Care Grant to non-South African children because of the required paper work.

Maintenance grant

The maintenance grant is yet another source of income directly affecting women. Women are often the primary caregivers of children, including those born out of wedlock. However, the maintenance grant is not a grant provided by the state but is paid from one person to another. The state's role is to ensure that it is paid.

The grant provision is based on the premise that both parents are obliged and are expected to contribute financially for their children. In cases of divorce, the court decides which party is responsible for monthly payments to secure the child's upkeep. Maintenance can be paid for children up to the age of 21

years or until the child is self-supporting. It is an obligatory requirement of all parents. Even when an unmarried man is not living with a woman, he is obliged to pay maintenance money once the paternity is established. If the children should stay with the father, the mother is equally under obligation to pay maintenance for the children to the father. This is one of the laws that is gender conscious.

There are, however, many problems confronting the parental maintenance system in South Africa. For this reason, "maintenance" is a specific area of concern for South African women.[185] The following concerns are often raised: [186]

+ There is widespread lack of responsibility shown by many liable parents in terms of their responsibility to support their dependents, especially where children are brought up in single parent households.
+ There is a perception among some non-custodial parents that custodial parents "abuse" the money they receive and spend it on themselves rather than their children.
+ There is a shortage of financial resources allocated to the maintenance system.
+ There is a lack of personnel to deal with the vast number of maintenance cases and the lengthy delays.
+ Other problems relate to the actual amount of maintenance to be paid by non-custodial parents. There are low and inadequate levels of awards in parental maintenance. Great variations exist between courts as to the monthly amount which is awarded.
+ There is also lack of proper tracing agents to locate liable persons and obtain accurate information about their income and means. The Maintenance Act does not address the

problem of those who are self-employed or in the informal sector, and whose financial state is often difficult to ascertain.

Despite the legal and moral duty on the part of both parents to provide for their child / children, many parents fail to do so, with the result that there is a large sector of children that do not receive the necessary financial assistance through the maintenance system. The State's duty to provide enters the picture only when parents are unable to provide – not because they do not want to.

Public works programmes
The Working for Water (WfW) programme is one of the South African government's public works programmes. One such programme is the *Tsitsikama* project Water For Work programme (WfW) programme which has a strong focus on the employment of women. The programme sets a target of 60 percent women employees. The workers interviewed expressed their views on employing women in the project. There was a clear awareness of the multiple roles women play and the importance of their income into these households.

Old age pension
Women over 60 years, and men over 65 years of age, receive a state old age grant of R570 per month. The grant is the largest current social security transfer and for those who receive it, the grant plays a pivotal poverty alleviation role for the entire household.

A review of the impact of government programmes reveals that the primary impact of government programmes on the aged has been in the area of income due to the provision of social grants. The proportion of women over 60 years[187] with no income has declined by almost five percent from 20 percent to 15 percent, whilst the proportion of women over 65 years[188] with no income has declined by four percent from 16 percent to 12 percent.

This improvement has been more pronounced for Black women. Nonetheless, a significant number of the aged remain outside the social security net. Significantly, the *Ingxoxo Zama-khosikazi* (Conversations among women) recommended that the eligibility for old age pension be extended to women who are 55 years old. The intention here is to extend the reach of the grant because in reality the old age pension is the sole income for a substantial number of households.

Programmes to alleviate poverty
Whilst women have celebrated the government driven initiatives aimed at improving the quality of life and status of women, their major concern has been the absence of a clearly defined development strategy for women. An emerging debate is whether the current welfare strategy, characterised by social grants, is consistent with a development and social transformation.

Despite a cohesive development approach, a number of best practices have emerged in sectors. However, as these are not effectively co-ordinated, it is not possible to provide a conclusive account on the impact of a poverty reduction strategy addressing women, nor to effectively monitor the impact of such a strategy on the lives of women, specifically "the poorest who live in rural areas, with incomes below the poverty lines.[189]

Since 2001, the recommendation has expanded to refer to a broader development fund for women (that is, to address the development needs of all South African women, and not only women entrepreneurs).

The letter written by Zanele Mbeki and Brigalia Bam (Co-Chairpersons of the South African Women in Dialogue) and add-

Programmes for Income Generation to Alleviate Poverty Among Women	Table 26
Department	**Programme in Place**
Department of Environmental Affairs	◆ The National Biodiversity Strategy and Action Plan which falls under the Department of Environmental Affairs benefits women by ensuring the sustainable use and development of the country's rich natural resources.Programmes and projects benefit women, particularly those aimed at poverty relief and economic empowerment. ◆ The transformation strategy of the fishing industry has made an impact towards women empowerment by supporting women entrepreneurs in this industry. ◆ The department, through the strategies of its implementing agency South African National Parks, ensures thatwomen benefit from its services by increasing the participation of marginalised and local people in its cooperative management.
Department of Technology	◆ The department has a project, which focuses on initiatives within the Poverty Relief, Infrastructure Investment and Job Creation Programme. The department's focus has been mainly on rural development, focusing on the transfer of available technologies to communities to enhance the use of local resources and indigenous knowledge to stimulate economic activity. Many of these projects have been implemented in poverty nodes as identified by the Integrated Sustainable Rural Development Programme (ISRDP). Technology partners follow a holistic approach to poverty relief, focusing on technology as one component to contribute towards economic empowerment of previously marginalised groups and communities, with special emphasis on women. A total of 112 projects are ongoing, ranging from bee keeping to papermaking and food production. A total of 1,459 women benefited from the projects.
Department of Minerals	◆ The department has projects that assist rural craft women to add value to their craft by mixing precious minerals into their products , So faras to increase the price in order to achieve sustainability. 16 groups of women have been established throughout the country, trained and assisted to set up to projects to manufacture precious minerals. The training was in the manufacturing of jewellery using traditional indigenous South Africa jewellery techniques, as well as in manufacturing non-ferrous and precious metal jewellery using hand tools and basic jewellery equipment. One hundred and forty three (143) women have gone through this process and some groups have begun to generate income averaging R1,000.00 per month. ◆ Women in Oil and Energy South Africa (WOESA) aims to expose and build the capacity of women to be empowered to participate in the energy sector. ◆ South African Women in Mining Association (SAWIMA) was established in 2003 with the aim of exposing and building the capacity of women so that they can be empowered to participate in the mining sector. A workshop on nuclear energy was organised to launch Women in Nuclear South Africa (WINSA) in 2003. The department recognised the need to mobilise and support the involvement of women in the various fields of nuclear technology and application, and radiation protection. Taking into account the historical barriers to the participation of women in nuclear fields, WINSA's vision is to be the leading organisation promoting the participation of South African women in the various nuclear fields and supporting them to realise their full potential in these fields. Priorities are on creating databases, sharing developments in the various nuclear-related fields, career opportunities, skills development and training, and awareness raising. Through close collaborations and co-ordination of efforts, WINSA has started to reach schools and institutions of higher learning and encourage females towards science and technology career-paths. By targeting the younger generation at the various levels of education, it is hoped that a significant contribution can be made to the expansion of the country's pool of expertise in the fields of science and technology, thus creating the required critical mass from which to attract women into careers in nuclear-related fields and specialisation in the respective fields. ◆ Technology for Women in Business (TWIB) recognises, appreciates and motivates women to use technology in enhancing efficiency and effectiveness in their businesses. In 2003, TWIB focused on women in Renewable Energy and Jewellery.
Department of Water Affairs	◆ In the development of the Levhuvhu River Government Scheme, local women were trained in concrete technology, catering, bookkeeping, minute taking and facilitation. Those trained in concrete technology have been employed in the scheme, and local women catered for project meetings. In such initiatives, sustainability is a threat, and only co-operative governance could be a means for ensuring poverty alleviation in these areas after the completion of projects. ◆ The department has been supporting the Water for Food Movement, which is an association of rural women who use water-harnessing mechanisms, in order tohave sufficient water for their communal vegetable gardens.

SOURCE Information provided by the relevant National Departments, Gender Focal Points, to the OSW, 2003.

ressed to a large number of decision- and policy-makers in South Africa, further notes that "we do not have a national programme of this kind." In this regard, in their annual meeting held in July 2005, South African Women in Dialogue noted the recommendation of AU Heads of States that the AU Commission establish a development fund for Black Women. They therefore renewed their recommendation that a South African Women's Development Fund be established.

In addition to the Integrated Sustainable Rural Strategy, a number of programmes addressing poverty eradication exist at national, provincial and local level and are outlined in Table 26.

SOCIAL SERVICES
Housing
The quality of lives can be ascertained from people's access to and utilisation of services in respect of housing, energy sources, water access and usage as well as the ability to acquire household goods and access to communication technologies. In South Africa, the right to housing is entrenched in the 1996 Constitution, which states that: "Everyone has the right to adequate housing. The state must take reasonable legislative and other measures, within its available resources, to achieve the progressive realisation to this right." Sections 26 (1) and (2).

In accordance with these rights, government has developed a series of laws, policies and mechanisms to provide access to accommodation and permanent housing. Initially, the Reconstruction and Development Programme (RDP) set a goal of 300,000 houses per annum to alleviate this dire need to proper housing for the majority of the people. It also planned to provide one million low-cost housing within the first five years of democracy.

In accordance with the provisions of the Constitution, the Housing Act of 1997 was passed to promote amongst others, the active participation of women in housing. The Act also created the opportunity for women to actively participate in the industry itself by availing the opportunity to access grants for bridging finance.

Redressing past inequalities in housing
In attempting to address the needs of the poor for housing and shelter, the following programmes have been put in place :[190]

- Subsidy for persons with disabilities. Disabled people who qualify obtain a housing subsidy amounting to R25,590, plus additional funds for special additions to their homes such as paving and ramps to their doors, grab rails in bath rooms, kick plates to doors and visible door bells for the deaf;
- Consolidation subsidy. For people living in an area on a serviced stand that government sold to them, a subsidy of R12,521 can be obtained for building a top structure or for the enhancement of an existing house on the property;
- Individual subsidies. These subsidies are available to individual beneficiaries who wish to buy an existing house or a stand linked to a house building contract in the market;
- Institutional subsidies. These subsidies are given to an approved housing institution. The institutions receive R23,100 per housing unit or family earning below R3,500 per month;
- Project Linked Subsidies. These are houses built by contractors, employed by the province or municipality, for groups of people that qualify for subsidies. The subsidy amount is linked to income and the beneficiary must finance any shortfall;
- Rural Housing Loan Fund. This fund focuses on providing loans, through intermediaries,

to low-income households for incremental housing purposes. Incremental housing is a people-driven process and this fund therefore seeks to empower low-income families in rural areas to access credit that enables them to build and improve their shelters;

♦ Relocation assistance. This subsidy is offered to borrowers from banks who, on 31 August 1997, were at least three months in arrears in payments of instalments and who need to be relocated to more affordable housing. The Department of Hou-sing in partnership with the Banking Council has established a company called SER-VON Housing Solutions (Pty) Ltd to mediate the awarding of the relocating grant as part of the strategy to normalise the housing environment;

♦ People's housing process. This subsidy is given to people who want to build their own homes. People are in charge of their own house construction process and are supported by a support organisation.

The Government introduced the principle that subsidy beneficiaries must contribute towards achieving access to the benefits of the housing subsidy. Thus, as of April 2002, all subsidy beneficiaries were required to make a contribution (of R2,479).

Significantly, the following sectors are exempt from making the contribution:

♦ The aged, the disabled and health stricken beneficiaries, provided they earn less than R800 per month.
♦ Beneficiaries of rural subsidies.
♦ Beneficiaries of an approved People's Housing Process.
♦ Beneficiaries who get government houses through emergency situations.

The beneficiaries include both male- and female-headed households with 61 percent and 39 percent receiving them, respectively. In an attempt to address the gender bias in housing ownership, female-headed households were specifically targeted to receive subsidies.

Clean and safe water
Since 2000, the government has initiated a programme to provide poor households with a basic supply of 6000 litres of water free of charge.cxcii Census 2001 indicates that 32.3 percent of the entire population receives water piped into their dwelling, 29 percent have water piped into their yards and 10.7 percent have water piped less then 200 metres away.

LAND
The South African White Paper on Land Reform specifically states that all laws that continue to discriminate against women need to be removed. Further, the White Paper provides for the removal of all legislative restrictions on women's access to land use. It compels government to put into place procedures meant to promote women's participation in decision-making, and emphasises that the purpose of land reform is to bring about equitable opportunities for both women and men. It makes the point however, that priority must be given to women. In this regard, a sectoral Land Reform Gender Policy[193] aims to create an enabling environment for women to access, own, control, use and manage land, as well as access credit for productive use of land.

There has been extensive legal reform in the area of land, with land and property rights for women being part of the discourse of justice for women in South Africa. In an effort to redress land rights, the Depart-ment of Land Affairs (DLA) introduced a series of land reform policies. These were aimed both at the alleviation of poverty and to address the injustices of the past. The land reform policy is based on three key concepts of restitution, redistribution and tenure and aims to achieve the following:

+ Compensate or restore land disposed by racially discriminatory practices and legislation put into place after 19 July 1913;
+ Provide people, especially women with tenure security;
+ Provide the poor with land for residential and productive purposes;

Enable the poor, labour tenants, farm workers and women to become beneficiaries of tenure reform programmes. Women make up a large proportion of farm workers and labour tenants, and are beginning to emerge as farm owners.

The policy of the DLA[194] emphasised the removal of legal restrictions on women's access to land, including marriage, inheritance and customary laws, gender equity in land access and effective participation of women in decision-making procedures. It committed the DLA to promoting the use of "gender sensitive participatory methodologies in project identification and planning."[195]

The DLA also adopted the "Land Reform Gender Policy Framework" in 1997, which 'aimed at creating an enabling environment for women to access, own, control, use and manage land; as well as access credit for productive use of the land."[196] The document outlined a set of guiding principles in relation to supporting gender equity in land reform.

In terms of policy and law, women have equal access to land in freehold areas. In practice, male control still continues in many areas. Land restitution has often meant that the ownership and control of land reverts back to the men and not necessarily to women.[197]

After the 1999 elections the state's priorities for land redistribution shifted more narrowly towards economic outcomes, and land reform policy shifted to support

black access to the commercial agricultural sector.[198] Beneficiaries of land reform were determined on criteria of race or historical disadvantage, rather than poverty or need (or gender). Research has suggested that although the new policy did not erect formal policy barriers for poor women, it had not "successfully addressed questions of how to target the poor in general ... and poor rural women ... particularly."[199]

The Department of Land Affairs reports that 137,521 households benefited from the Land Redistribution and Tenure Reform Programmes, of which 17,482 (i.e. 12.71 percent) beneficiaries were female-headed households, during the period 1994 to March 2003.[200]

The land reform policy was designed to give women security and equal rights with men with regard to ownership, control and use of land. However, land reform measures have not achieved major shifts in access and ownership, especially to and for women. Very little land has been redistributed or transferred and gender equity has not been reached in terms of land reform. For many rural women, land is a means of survival and a vital productive resource. It becomes a valuable commodity in times of rural crisis and high urban unemployment. In most instances, women do not have large pieces of land as they are often close to home because of their social and domestic responsibilities as homemakers, child minders and caretakers of the sick and the elderly.

Women are therefore often found in community garden projects – gardening pockets of land near the homestead. Their priorities are also to have taps in/or near the homestead. In this regard, the land reform measures hold certain challenges for government to make them more inclusive of women's needs and to address the gendered nature of poverty in the country. In addition to policy shift, research has also suggested that the gap between policy and practice in relation to women has persisted, largely due to "the lack of accountability by DLA management for their Gender Policy; secondly, and linked to that, the weakness of the women's movement in the rural areas, and thirdly, conceptual shortcomings in the way in which gender equality and women's rights have been understood."[201]

Clearly, there are problems with the National Land Restitution and Tenure Reform programmes. The major contention is that the Restitution of Land Rights Act 22 of 1994 aims to restore land rights to those who had access to land before. Despite the progressive intention of the Act, which states that priority must be given to those with the most pressing needs, it is more likely that restitution may disadvantage women, as they had not traditionally owned land.

ENVIRONMENT

Legislation and policy governing environmental issues in South Africa recognise women as important primary stakeholders and thus provide for women empowerment issues.

The National Environment Management Act 107 of 1998 recognises the role that women and youth play in environmental management and that their participation should be promoted. This Act, together with the White Paper on Integrated Pollution and Waste Management, acknowledges that women, especially in the rural areas, are the traditional custodians of natural resources. As such, these policy frameworks call for the encouragement and support of women's participation in the design, planning and implementation of environmental programmes and projects, integrated pollution and waste management education and capacity-building programmes and projects.

The Law Reform Programme, which is aimed at developing an integrated and coherent code of environmental management that promotes sustainable development, ensures that the needs of women and children are included within the various pieces of environmental legislation.

The South African Framework on the Promotion and Development of Tourism acknowledges that women, particularly those living in rural areas, can and should play a crucial role in the new tourism drive of the country. This policy framework encourages the participation of women as decision-makers and implementers of awareness programmes and community-based programmes in the tourism industry. Furthermore, this policy framework makes provision for support measures for women entrepreneurs in the tourism industry.

All environmental programmes ensure that the principles of Agenda 21, including the principle of including women as decision-makers and beneficiaries in all matters pertaining to sustainable development, is taken into consideration during programme planning and implementation.

The National Biodiversity Strategy and Action Plan indirectly benefits women by ensuring the sustainable use and development of the country's rich natural resources. Women are identified as beneficiaries of programmes and projects aimed at poverty relief and economic empowerment. Furthermore, the transformation strategy of the fishing industry has made an impact towards women empowerment by supporting women entrepreneurs in this industry.

The Department of Environmental Affairs and Tourism through the strategies of its implementing agency South African National Parks, specifically promotes women participation in its cooperative management, equitable use of natural resources and benefit sharing.

The provisions of this policy framework are translated into programmes and projects mainly by the department's provincial line function departments. However, a major challenge is a lack of national sector specific gender equality and women's specific strategy to ensure uniform implementation of provisions aimed at women's empowerment by all role-players.

HEALTH

In the 1997 White Paper on the Transformation of the Health System, women were identified as a priority group, with an emphasis on women's empowerment, socioeconomic status, equality and autonomy. Within the overall transformation of the health system, maternal, child and women's health was recognised as priority by the government and an integral part of primary healthcare. The White Paper provided that the Department of Health would ensure the allocation of adequate resources to provide comprehensive and integrated health services (with women accessing a "one-stop shop" of services).

A key component in this was the recognition of women's reproductive rights. In addition, the White Paper emphasised the accessibility of health services to "the rural and the urban poor" and farm workers.[202]

Under this programme, government has facilitated women's access to health and related services, including right to family planning, health information, and HIV and AIDS prevention. Pregnant women and children under the age of seven have access to free medical care, while safe and free termination of pregnancy is guaranteed during the first 12 weeks of pregnancy.[203] Increased awareness of

HIV among women and girls is being promoted by both government and NGOs, and national campaigns on the awareness to cervical and breast cancer have increased.

This approach is entrenched in the 1996 South African Constitution which saw a guarantee of women's reproductive freedom and access to healthcare services, including reproductive healthcare. It is also reflected in the provision of free maternal and child healthcare from 1994.

In line with problems across the health system, implementation of policies and programmes has taken time and access to healthcare has been uneven across the country. Much of this has been due to the major restructuring of national and provincial departments and at local level occasioned by the fundamental policy shifts from 1994.

The inherited inequities of the apartheid system and the ongoing challenges of transformation have meant that policy development and implementation needed to focus on institutional transformation and the re-allocation of resources to deliver effective services, as well as more substantive issues such as women's health.

In 2000, the government's Department of Health developed a Strategic Framework and set out a 10-point strategy that envisioned amongst others:
- The re-organisation of support services;
- Legislative reform;
- Improving the quality of care;
- The revitalisation of hospital services;
- The speeding up of delivery of an essential package of services through the district health system; and
- Decreasing of the morbidity and mortality rates through strategic interventions.

New legislation has since been passed and some of the legislative reforms hold specific advantages to women's health. These legislative imperatives aim to:

+ Make drugs more affordable and promote the use of generic equivalents;
+ Regulate the medical schemes industry to prevent it from discriminating against "high risk" individuals like the aged and sick;
+ Legalise abortion and allow for safe access to it in both the public and private health facilities; and
+ Limit smoking in public places and make the public aware of the health risks of tobacco by placing restrictions on tobacco advertisements.

In this context, it has become increasingly clear that transformation can be a time-consuming process and a significant challenge to human and financial resources, as well as capacity. It still needs to be met for full and effective policy development and implementation.[204]

The health sector still continues to face challenges of unevenness in service provision where quality of service is affected by inadequate resource allocation as well as the prohibitive cost of medication for the majority of the population.[205]

Maternity leave benefits
With regard to maternity leave benefits, the 1999 study on Gender and the Private Sector revealed that 72 percent of the South African companies sampled were complying with the Labour Relations Act regulations in terms of maternity leave. Seventeen percent of respondents indicated that they provide unpaid maternity leave for periods ranging from one to three months, while 41 percent provide paid maternity leave for three months and 21 percent for six months. It also revealed that an alarming 41 percent of responding companies did not have a sexual harassment policy. Only 55 percent indicated that they have a policy on sexual harassment and four percent indicated

that they were currently formulating one.

The Labour Relations Act, No 66 of 1995 provides that a Code of Good Practice had to be developed for the workplace. The premise of such a code is to make the work environment gender-friendly. In 1998, the Code of Good Practice on the Handling of Sexual Harassment Cases was published to ensure the elimination of sexual harassment in the workplace.

This was one of the first visible "hard" affirmative action positions taken by national government to ensure a safe and secure working environment for women and men. It was also compulsory that all institutions should adopt or adapt the Code of Good Conduct in their work policies.

Abortion
Prior to 1996, legal abortion was available only in very restricted circumstances, and on recommendation by at least three doctors. Parliament adopted the Choice on Termination of Pregnancy Act (1996) which now makes it legal for the termination of pregnancy up to 12 weeks, between 13 and 20 weeks under certain conditions and upon recommendation by a medical practitioner or midwife. These conditions include the socio-economic situation of the woman, rape, incest and the health risk to the woman.

HIV AND AIDS
The primary source of policy on HIV and AIDS is the Department of Health's HIV, AIDS and STD Strategic Plan for South Africa.[206]

This established a broad policy outline for the period 2000-2005 and was "designed to guide the country's response to the epidemic."

The plan recognises the "vulnerable position of women in society" and states that it "shall be addressed to ensure that they do not suffer discrimination, nor remain unable to take effective measures to prevent infection" (para 4). However, gender is not fully integrated into the plan. Rather, women are treated as a set of vulnerable groups (mothers, survivors of violence, sex workers) that require special measures.

An example of the failure to mainstream women within the plan can be seen in the section on "Human Rights." This section calls for open discussion and a protective legal and policy environment, but does not mention women's rights, except in relation to "special groups" such as sex workers and victims of sexual assault.

Moreover, there is no immediate evidence of a gendered approach in the policy goals for treatment, care and support, or in relation to education about safer sex behaviour or youth. Although gender is not mainstreamed into the AIDS policy, the fact that it adopts a human rights approach means that there is space to engender specific plans and programmes.

The absence of an explicitly gendered policy is also reflected in the absence of gendered political leadership. There is insufficient evidence that the highest level of government is articulating a public political commitment to addressing the specific vulnerabilities and issues that HIV and AIDS pose for women.

Policies on prevention include the promotion of safer sex practices (although not gendered); the promotion of improved health-seeking behaviour (although not gendered); improving access to male and female condoms; and reducing parent to child transmission by improving access to voluntary counselling and testing (VCT), family planning, developing clinical guidelines for reducing transmission at child-birth and rolling out a package of service including anti-retroviral therapy to HIV positive pregnant women. The plan committed to investigate options for appropriate post-exposure services for victims of sexual abuse.

In terms of HIV and AIDS more needs to be done to identify and deal with interfaces between them and other variables such as gender-based violence and sexuality issues and violence.[207]

The HIV, AIDS and STD Strategic Plan for South Africa, 2000-2005 recognises that the imbalances and inequalities between women and men have placed women in a position of being unable to negotiate safer sexual practices with their partners. It acknowledges that the social vulnerability of women should be addressed in order to ensure that women do not suffer discrimination, nor remain unable to take effective measures to prevent infection'. Nonetheless, the gendered dimensions of the epidemic are not sufficiently considered.

The Plan treats women as a vulnerable group compromising mothers, survivors of violence and sex workers who require special measures. An example of the failure to mainstream women within the Plan can be seen in the section on 'Human Rights'. This section calls for open discussion and a protective legal and policy environment, but does not mention women's rights, except in relation to sex workers and victims of sexual assault. Moreover, there is no immediate evidence of a gendered approach in the policy goals for treatment, care and support, or in relation to education about safe sex behaviour or youth.

The Plan encourages the "women's sector" to develop its own policies. This seems to reinforce the marginalisation of women, rather than acknowledge the need to integrate or mainstream gender (the differing interests and needs of women and men) into all aspects of policy.

This results in policy gaps and silences. For example, it is not obvious from the Plan that an understanding of human rights includes women's sexual rights or equality or bodily integrity in negotiating safer sex – or that young girls will be prioritised in a particular way in policies relating to youth. Issues such as socio-cultural practices that impact on women's vulnerability are not addressed.

Development and implementation of policy on STIs has been both participatory and relatively effective since 1990. It has also been characterised by strong national and international linkages and effective use of government and non-government expertise.

A National Strategy for the control and management of STIs was introduced by the Department of Health in the latter 1990s. This was done in collaboration with a broad spectrum of stakeholders and based on the World Health Organisation's (WHO) recommended approach to STIs referred to as "syndromic management." This resulted in amending the National STI Treatment Guidelines to include:

+ Safer sex education;
+ Condom promotion; and
+ Partner notification and treatment.

SOCIAL WELFARE
Violence
There are several ongoing initiatives on sexual assault and rape. In 2002, cabinet approved an "Anti-Rape Strategic Framework" that calls for a balanced approach in dealing with victims and perpetrators and which sets out short-, medium- and long-term policy objectives. This affects six government departments. Victim empowerment initiatives and special police units and sexual offences courts have begun to improve the response of the criminal justice system to such crimes. In addition, a victim empowerment programme that addresses the needs of survivors has been established. Special police units and sexual offences courts have been set up and the substantive and procedural law on sexual offences is subject to review. At the time of writing the Sexual Offences Bill is before Parliament.

In seeking to address the intersection of HIV and violence, government has tended to focus on rape survivors. Post exposure prophylaxis is being rolled out and the Sexual Offences Bill contains provisions relating to this and the testing of alleged offenders.

Violence in schools
In different provinces, Departments of Education have made concerted efforts to address the increasing violence at schools. However, violence in the schools remains a problem although the Constitution enshrines the fundamental human rights principle of bodily and psychological integrity. Violence in schools is a direct violation of this basic human right. Since the Human Rights Watch[208] released their research report "Scared at School: Sexual Violence against Girls in South African schools," the problem of harassment, other forms of gender-based violence, sexually transmitted diseases and the increase of HIV and AIDS amongst young girls have been highlighted.

In general, government has adopted a multi-faceted and integrated approach to raise awareness and improve service delivery to combat violence against women. National awareness campaigns, like the 16 Days of Activism against Violence against Women and Children, have received growing support from across society. However, violence remains endemic in South Africa, embedded in patriarchal norms. It will take concerted effort by the state and society to stem the tide.

State responses to gender-based violence

In general, reducing violence against women is one of the key priorities of the South African government, affecting the work of many government departments, including the Departments of Justice, Safety and Security, Health and Social Development and the National Prosecution Authority. South Africa has made extensive progress in the development of policies, laws and plans and the identification of institutional mechanisms. However, problems of implementation are substantial. In addition, much of the efforts are directed at addressing the problem of violence after it occurs, rather than focussing on prevention.

In the area of domestic violence, government passed the Domestic Violence Act, 116 of 1998, a review of an earlier 1992 Act widely hailed as a "best practice" law. It provides women with a relatively simple and accessible procedure for obtaining an interdict against their abusive partners. The law has a broad reach to include physical, psychological and economic violence, as well as persons who live in same sex relationships and extended families. The Act has suffered extensive problems of implementation. These include:

+ The difficulties of intersecting oral co-ordination of implementation, especially between the police and the courts;
+ The obligation to assist and report cases of victims/survivors of domestic violence is not placed on the health sector;
+ The lack of support systems outside the criminal justice system. The need for shelters is pressing;
+ The lack of resources at magistrates courts and police stations;
+ The attitudes of personnel at law enforcement facilities; and
+ The role of culture and patriarchy.

The Act assumes that women will report violence in relationships and will approach the courts. Yet, there remain multiple reasons why this will not occur, including the stigma attached to this and the social norms and economic imperatives that keep women in abusive relationships. The reach of the law is limited and a purely legal response to a social phenomenon such as domestic violence is insufficient for real social transformation.

Sexual harassment[209]

Sexual harassment remains a problem in the workplace, schools and in public places. Advances in technology have also opened the way to new forms of stalking and worrying acts of sexual aggression, which challenge current and conventional forms of addressing gender-based violence. Harassment in schools is an area of concern. Independent studies report a high prevalence of sexual violence in schools and estimate reporting of such incidences at 34 percent.[210]

Sexual harassment at the workplace is the purview of the Department of Labour, specifically the Commission for Conciliation, Mediation and Arbitration, and the Labour Court (which falls under the Department of Justice). Laws passed to protect women (and others) against violence in the workplace include the Employment Equity Act 55 of 1998, which recognises the harassment of an employee as a form of unfair discrimination. This is accompanied by the Code of Good Practice on the Handling of Sexual Harassment issued in terms of the Labour Relations Act.

Further legislation addressing sexual harassment includes:

+ The Promotion of Equality and Prevention of Unfair Discrimination Act, No. 4 of 2000;
+ The Employment of Educators Act, No. 53 of 1998, amended in 2000, which explicitly makes sexual harassment a form of serious misconduct (Section 17); and

- The South African Schools Act, No. 84 of 1996, under which sexual harassment constitutes misconduct.

The Department of Justice has developed a plan for the rollout of equality courts that would be able to hear cases of sexual harassment,[211] in terms of the Promotion of Equality and Prevention of Unfair Discrimination Act.

Child prostitution

It is important to note that child prostitution is prohibited under the Sexual Offences Act, No. 23 of 1957, and the Child Act No. 75 of 1982. Both Acts have been reviewed by the South African Law Commission, and the recommended reforms are yet to be passed by Parliament. Further, the Sexual Offences Bill, and the Film and Publications Act, No. 56 of 1996 regulate pornography.

Trafficking in women and girls

An emerging concern within the area of gender-based violence is the issue of trafficking of women and children. Currently, South Africa has no specific legislation addressing trafficking. However, the South African law Commission is working on a comprehensive issue paper on trafficking. Work done by the Office on the Status of Women in preparation for South Africa's participation[212] in the 47th Session of the UN Commission of the Status of Women revealed the following, with regard to trafficking in women in South Africa.

- South Africa is both a transit, and destination point for trafficking in women. The extent to which South Africa is a source (starting point) for trafficking is more difficult to determine and much work needs to be done to determine the extent to which women and children are trafficked into/ and through South Africa and the exact reasons (sexual, domestic or other forms of labour and/or marriage).

- The absence of specific legislation addressing trafficking hampers both the effective protection of trafficked persons and the prosecution of offenders.
- To a large extent, persons who are trafficked into South Africa are treated as "illegal immigrants" and are therefore deported. This applies both to children and adults. The implication is that persons who are trafficked, can be re-trafficked into South Africa and, indeed, often are.
- There are clear indications of intra-country trafficking, that is, trafficking of children specifically within the country, mostly from rural to urban metropolises. This is an area where international instruments do not apply. However, this area needs much attention.

Legal framework

Despite the gaps in policy and legislation, some work has been done

- In its review of the Sexual Offences Act, (yet to be passed by Parliament) the South African Law Commission has dedicated a chapter to trafficking in a section entitled "Sexual Offence: Adult Protection".[213]
- Trafficking in children is addressed in the Sexual Offences Bill and the Children's Bill yet to be addressed by Parliament.

South Africa has signed the following international instruments wh-ich address trafficking in persons:

- The UN Convention Against Transnational Crime; and
- The Protocol to Prevent, Suppress and Punish Trafficking in Persons, especially Women and Children.

Although, as stated above, South Africa currently does not have specific anti-trafficking legislation, various legal remedies can be applied by law enforcement authorities to prosecute offences relating to the trafficking in persons and/ or to protect the victims of trafficking. These include:

+ The Prevention of Organised Crime Act, No. 121 of 1998;
+ The Refugees Act, No. 130 of 1998;
+ The Domestic Violence Act, No. 116 of 1998;
+ The Sexual Offences Act, No. 23 of 1957;
+ The Basic Conditions of Employment Act, No 75 of 1997; and
+ The Child Care Amendment Act, No 96 of 1996.

It is important to note however that these laws do not address all aspects of trafficking in persons and contains various loopholes that hamper the proper protection of trafficked persons and the effective prosecution of offenders.

EDUCATION
Legislative framework
Government has instituted legislation to transform education as illustrated in Table 27.

Legislative Framework for Education	Table 27
Legislation	**Summary**
The Constitution of South Africa, 1996	States that everyone has the right to a basic education, including adult basic education, and to further education, which the state, through reasonable measures, must make progressively available and accessible.
The National Education Policy Act 27 of 1996	Provides for redressing the inequalities of the past in educational provisions, including the promotion of gender equality and the advancement of the status of women.
The Skills Development Act 97 of 1998	This Act does not specifically address the training needs of women but states that the Department of Labour has to ensure that it gives effect to the provisions of the Beijing Platform of Action.
The Adult Basic Education and Training Act of 2000	Regulates basic education for older persons who have been denied opportunities of education.
The South African Schools Act of 1996	This Act regulates the admission of learners to public schools to ensure that the girl-child receives basic education. To this end, it provides that a public school must admit learners and serve their educational requirements without any discrimination.
The Further Education and Training Act of 1998	This Act governs education at the tertiary level and makes provision to address the advancement of women towards higher education, particularly in previously male-dominated fields of study.

SOURCE Office on the Status of Women, 2006.

Increasing access and opportunities for the girl-child to education
Government has implemented specific programmes that increased the access and opportunities for the girl-child to education, especially in mathematics and science. A further concern is that women are under-represented in the senior echelons of the academic institutions.[214] Historically, education has been extremely racialised and gendered. The new democratic government is faced with this daunting task to "fix" and unify the severely fragmented and racialised education system.

The curriculum has been transformed to make it more relevant to the needs of citizens. The Revised National Curriculum Statement (RNCS) includes the revised learning area of Life Orientation to enable all learners to become competent in life skills and in dealing with health and social development issues such as teenage pregnancies and HIV and AIDS.

Advancing women and the girl-child in science and technology
Initiatives to advance women and the girl-child in science and technology education include the following:

+ Establishment of 102 schools, which are awarded "Centres of Excellence" status for teaching Maths, and Science. These schools are appropriately resourced for this purpose.[215]
+ The National Science and Technology Programme,[216] a two-week-long "science camp" for young female learners was hosted in 2002 by the Department of Science and Technology. The aim of this programme was to provide the girl-child with opportunities to engage in innovative and participatory programmes in the science and technology field, with a view to highlighting gender disparities in the field as well as creating enthusiasm for career choices within scientific

fields. A total of 347 female learners benefited from the programme which focused on four main themes: HIV and AIDS, Space Science, Biodiversity and Engineering.

Addressing poor representation of women within the Information Technology (IT) sector. In addressing this challenge, the Department of Communications has undertaken to improve skills development, especially for women, within this sector through the establishment of the Institute for Satellite and Software Applications (ISSA).[217] The aim is to provide tuition in industry-related studies for female students from disadvantaged backgrounds. In 2000, the Institute reflected a 100 percent women enrolment for a Masters Degree in Software Engineering, while 54 percent women were studying for a Masters Degree in Engineering Science.[218]

Skills development

Government has enabled, through the Skills Development Act, for people to upgrade and/or acquire new skills necessary for employment and advancement in the labour force. In 2002, the proportion of women in the 15 years-and-over age group who acquired learning skills for work was 7.14 percent compared to 10.32 percent men.[219]

Policy on teenage pregnancy in schools

The education system has a policy on teenage pregnancy in schools. The policy ensures that the girl-child is protected from unfair dismissal from schools and from unfair victimisation. In addition, government has established a Directorate of Gender Equity within the Department of Education, which focuses on eradicating sex and gender-based violence and monitor gender-mainstreaming within the education sector.[220] It has also enacted legislation that obligates the private and public sectors to provide education and training in the workplace.[221] Further, it has improved enrolment and retention of young women in tertiary institutions.

However the following are still obstacles to women and girls education:

- Negative attitudes to the importance of educating girls persist in South Africa and these prevent girls from completing school;
- Teenage pregnancy rates are increasing and consequently girls leave school earlier compared to boys;
- Girls sometimes believe that they have a duty to help support the family and leave school in the hope that they'll find some form of employment;
- Sexual harassment and sexual violence against girls in schools is endemic and often hampers scholastic performance and results in school dropouts;[222] and
- Government provides minimal support for pre-schools and crèches. The education policy provides for one pre-school year for every child, but this is being introduced in a phased way and is not yet compulsory. Otherwise, there are small subsidies from the Departments of Welfare or municipalities for selected institutions. The absence of childcare facilities affects the ability of their parents and primary caregivers to engage in other activities.[223]

PART III
THE WAY FORWARD

This update of the 1997 *Beyond Inequalities Women in South Africa* book indicates that whilst some progress has been made in advancing gender equality, women's empowerment and justice, more still needs to be done and that areas in which progress has been made be consolidated so that gains are not lost.

This section of the report highlights priority areas of concern, challenges and actions that need to be taken by the South African government in order to achieve gender equality, women's empowerment and justice in the post-Beijing era, and in line with national, regional and international gender equality commitments.

PRIORITIES FOR FUTURE ACTION
National Gender Machinery

At the administrative level,[224] this remains a critical gap in advancing gender mainstreaming. At the policy level, a gender mainstreaming strategy has been adopted. However, appropriate "expertise" and "resources" have not been put in place to realise this. Thus, key national policies, including the National Strategic Plan on HIV and AIDS, the Integrated Rural Development Strategy and the Urban Renewal Strategy do not reflect a consideration of the gendered dimensions of the critical areas of concern.

The democratisation process has also brought on new challenges, which have a specific impact on women's lives, and will impact on government's ability to meet these needs. Among these are:

◆ The diminishing size of the household and the break-up of extended family structures, which translates into increased demands for housing and basic services;

◆ The changing nature of the economy and the increase in the numbers of women who fall within the category of those who are considered economically active. In addition women tend to be too dependent on job opportunities within the "public sector", and are often forced into survivalist enterprises within the informal sector;

◆ More women are migrating from rural areas into urban and peri-urban areas. Women who live in households with a pensioner are more likely to migrate; and

◆ The number of marriages is decreasing, with more women delaying marriages, but having children. This contributes to the rise of female-headed households.

Implementation of legal instruments

The years following South Africa's democracy have brought significant progress in the legal position of South African women and their protection under the law based upon a constitutional guarantee of gender equality. Yet, the anomalous situation pertains, where women continue to experience abuse and gender-based inequalities in the social, political, and economic aspects of their lives. Values that directly affect the treatment of women and frequently inhibit them from claiming their equal rights and accessing resources and opportunities prevail in society.

South Africa has developed its policies and legislations with regard to women from a rights-based approach. However, the slow implementation of the myri-

ad of progressive laws and policies tends to retard the advancement and empowerment of a large percentage of women. More legislation still needs to be passed.

+ The Customary Inheritance Bill, the Sexual Offences Bill and the Communal Land Rights Bill. Regarding the former two bills, despite the understanding based on the constitution that where there is a contradiction between the attainment of human rights and the practice of Customary Law, the emotive nature of these two pieces of legislation has meant that these have not been passed. The debates on the Communal Land Rights Bill reflect the concerns of women, who argue that the Bill continues to reflect the needs of male traditional leaders instead of women, and the slow pace of progress with regards to women's claims to ownership, and/ or control of land.

+ A pertinent theme is the need for education to inform, not only women on rights, but also to increase the awareness and knowledge of gender rights at all levels of society, including the workplace and schools.

Decision-making

During the last 10 years, major progress has been made in advancing women in political and decision-making positions at national and provincial government levels.

The slow advancement of women leaders at local council level is an area that requires attention.

The public sector has not reached its targeted quotas of women in decision-making and management positions.

The Judiciary, Armed Forces, Police Services and Foreign Service also remain areas of challenge.

The following are some challenges and areas needing action.

+ Neither the South African Constitution, nor the Electoral Act specifies a quota for women in Parliament or in Cabinet. This raises concerns regarding the sustainability of the gains of the first decade of democracy.

+ The requirements of transition have highlighted new capacity-challenges confronting all parliamentarians. However, it has been women parliamentarians who have articulated and, to some extent, attempted to highlight these in a coherent manner.[225] They include:
  o Institutional weaknesses;
  o Capacity development;
  o Balancing the dual role of parliamentary committee work and that of participating in parliamentary institutions put in place to advance women's empowerment through the work of Parliament and its Committees;
  o Accessing and/or assessing what constitutes adequate resources to enable meaningful gender mainstreaming of legislative processes;
  o Funding for the work of Parliamentary Committees has been a key challenge, with ongoing delays in reaching consensus on a viable funding system for Parliament;

+ It is important that voter education programmes be implemented to give the illiterate voters (the majority of whom are women) the opportunity to grasp complex electoral processes.[226] For women to be actively involved in the political processes, it is important that they change how they perceive themselves, change the way they relate to politics and bridge the growing gulf between women in parliament and women in society;

+ Voting stations, especially in rural areas, should be in convenient areas for women, free from harm, intimidation or violence; and

♦ It is also important that women be given the same opportunity as men to stand as candidates for elections.[227]

Local level governance

Since 1997, the Department of Local Government has hosted a series of conferences, focusing on women at local government level, a "Powerhouse for Transformation." These processes and the "conversations"[228] have pointed to the following:

♦ An absence of a clearly articulated policy framework, guiding women's empowerment and the realisation of gender equality at this level of government;

♦ The absence of an agreed national strategy for mainstreaming gender at this level of governance;

♦ Women in leadership positions at local governance level have expressed feelings of isolation and want strong mechanisms to support new entrants into leadership and management positions; and

♦ Skills development and capacity-building are required to enable councillors and managers to implement their roles in an effective manner. These would include training in governmental processes, procedures and policies.

Economy

Improving women's position in the economy requires structural transformation to increase overall equity and growth, rather than just better enforcement of anti-discrimination measures. Key steps are required that aim to:

♦ Shift the formal sector toward more labour-intensive methods that could provide employment on a large scale;

♦ Improve the ability of poor households to engage in the economy by providing productive assets, skills and access to marketing and financial net-

works, amongst others, through large-scale land reform as well as improved access to credit, infrastructure and training in black communities, with a focus on women;

♦ Reduce the burden of reproductive labour on women, both by improving household infrastructure and also by influencing the division of labour in the household, through education and by enhancing women's economic independence; and

♦ Ensure genuine equity in the education system in terms of class, race and region as well as gender, which would be reflected, at least in representative pass rates for Matric and in greater representation in the universities.

In addition, Government needs to pay attention to uneven service delivery and allocation of resources in sectors like health and justice, co-operation between government departments, and implementation of policy and legislation such as the gender and labour laws.

There is need to monitor developments and efforts dealing with the establishment of organisations at all levels, from community to government, through integrated and multi-faceted approaches to achieving equality for women.

Measures to end poverty

Anti-poverty measures should be reviewed to ensure that they contribute as far as possible to higher productivity and incomes at the household level, which in turn, requires affordable access to services at a level sufficient to engage with the economy.

♦ The government should do far more to support the growth of light industry and services. That involves developing a broad vision for growth in specific industries, and co-ordinating supply-side measures, skills development and infrastructure to achieve it. Critically, these industries should be geared to meeting basic needs and reducing the cost of living as well as increasing exports and replacing imports. Industries that could create employment, especially for women, include the public services; home-based personal services such as childcare, hairdressing or catering; the retail industry and tourism; transport; light manufacturing (assembly of appliances, food processing, clothing and textiles, furniture, plastics and so on); and industries downstream from metal and chemicals production.

- In the labour force, employment equity and decent conditions seem unlikely to work for most in the absence of stronger organisation. In sectors that are difficult for unions to regulate and monitor, it might be possible to consider mobilisation through service or community-based organisations.

- Existing anti-discrimination legislation, in particular the Employment Equity, Skills Development and Broad-Based Black Economic Empowerment Acts, should be reviewed systematically. The Employment Equity Act appears to have had little real impact on employment patterns, especially for lower-level workers. Given the inherited economic structure, anti-discrimination legislation necessarily ends up benefiting only the small high-level groups.

Enabling ownership of land by women[229]

Some of the steps, which need to be put in place to enable ownership of land by women, are the removal of legal restrictions on participation by women in land reform including:

- Reform of marriage, inheritance and customary law (which favour men and have obstacles to women receiving land);

- Establishing specific mechanisms to enable women to access financial and support services;
- Establishing specific mechanisms to provide security of tenure for women, including the registration of assets gained through land reform in the name of women as direct beneficiaries;
- Enabling, through gender training, all those involved in land reform to undertake gender analysis, which involves systematically examining the roles, relations and processes with a focus on power imbalances and access to resource;
- Facilitating the removal of legal restrictions on participation by women in land reform including establishing specific mechanisms to enable women to access financial and support services.

Access to financial resources

The removal of legal restrictions on participation by women in land reform including:

- Reform of marriage, inheritance and customary law (which favour men and contain obstacles to women receiving land);
- Specific mechanisms to enable women to access financial and support services;
- Specific mechanisms to provide security of tenure for women, including the registration of assets gained through land reform in the name of women as direct beneficiaries;
- Enabling all those involved in land reform to undertake gender analysis which involves systematically examining the roles, relations and processes with a focus on power imbalances and access to resources; and
- A monitoring and evaluation system for the land reform programmes which provides information necessary for mo-nitoring women's participation.

Education

Despite advancements made in achieving some levels of gender equality in education, gaps remain. The following areas still need to be addressed:

- Increase female enrolments in non-traditional subject areas such as science and technology and in engineering at tertiary and university levels;
- Increase the training in employment of women in non-traditional subject areas; and
- Increase the representation of women within the IT sector.

Measures to end violence against women

South Africa has instituted large-scale initiatives, both at the advocacy, policy and legislative level to address gender-based violence. However, the following remain as challenges and areas of priority:

- Effective and comprehensive training for magistrates, prosecutors, court clerks, police officers, health workers, social workers and prison officials;
- Addressing the various roles of all the above stakeholders in the implementation of the Act;
- Decrease the high levels of violence in educational institutions.

Gender and media

The media and information sector still has to deal with some challenges:

- Continued negative representation of women in the media;
- Violation of women's bodies in some of the images of women in the media;
- Exploitation of women's sexuality;
- Pornographic channels and balancing this with freedom of expression.
- Celebration of the culture of violence, violation and mutilation in films and music;
- Increasing sexist advertisements;

- Reportage of issues affecting women's lives – lack of interest in these issues and negative projection of women in leadership;
- Under-representation of women in positions of management in the media (editors and senior political writers); and
- Absence or inadequate covering of rural women's (and poor people's) stories and lives.

Information Communication Technologies

The Information Communication Technology (ICT) sector faces, among other challenges, inadequate infrastructure and lack of access, particularly by poor women. The following areas therefore need to be focused on:

- The development of basic infrastructure such as, roads, electrification, transportation and other basic services, which have a direct impact on the accessibility of technology;
- Inadequate skills and lack of familiarity with technology, especially among women in poor communities;
- Ensuring security at multi-purpose centres, especially for the equipment;
- Engaging in consultation with communities in setting up the multi-purpose centres and other projects for provision of technology. Communities need to be part of the decision-making process, including needs assessment, and setting up of priority areas and in project development;
- Adopting an integrated approach to development at all times;
- Marketing of community services. Often, community projects, which are set up, are not properly promoted and therefore under utilised; and
- Poverty still affects the extent to which communities can have access to technology.

CHALLENGES

Women made their mark, to a greater extent, prior to 1994 through NGOs. However, there has been a steady decline of women's NGOs after the ushering in of a new democratic order. Significantly, women are strong participants in the democratisation process, with women constituting the largest percentage in the electoral processes to date.

With the decline in women's rights-based organisations, as well as women's participation in civic organisations, it is argued by some, "the women's movement has abdicated the responsibility for women's rights to the state." Currently, South Africa does not have a women's coalition, or umbrella body articulating, co-ordinating or advancing a women's rights agenda within the broader civil society formations, a position that has not changed since the last report was written.

Civil activism around issues of violence against women, issues of a basic income grant, the proper implementation and monitoring of the Domestic Violence Act is continuing. Civil society argues that the issues of justice are not properly addressed because of the inadequacy of the bureaucratic state. Black women in rural and peri-urban areas remain marginalised and dispossessed. Emergent concerns are discern-able, including vulnerable women and children, namely, scho-olgirls, rural women, poor women, those living with HIV and AIDS, abused women and displaced women. The repercussions of gender violence are extensive.

Arguably, however, there is some co-ordination amongst the NGOs addressing gender-based violence, and a nascent movement of men as partners in advancing gender equality. When South Africa presented its report to the CEDAW Committee in 1998, the Committee commended South African women, though he majority in most organised formations, including faith-based organisations and the electorate, have yet to harness their power to define and articulate a national programme for the advancement of women.

CONCLUSION

The report has highlighted initiatives in addressing perceived needs in women's lives. These have been achieved to various degrees in different sectors. However, the report also illustrates new trends emerging in women's lives and points to new challenges, both at policy and programme level. The litmus test for government in the next 10 years would be on whether the prioritisation and monitoring processes factor these developments into the formulation of government programmes and policies.

PART IV
REFERENCES AND BIBLIOGRAPHY

Endnotes

1 President T. Mbeki, State of the Nation Address, 14 February 2003.
2 SADC Declaration on Gender and Development sets the target for the achievement of at least 30 percent of women in political and decision-making structures by the year 2005.
3 National Report on Ten Years of Freedom by the Presidency, Office on the Status of Women (draft), submitted to the SADC Gender Equity Unit, 2004.
4 Government of South Africa, South African Millennium Development Goals Report Goals, 2005.
5 Ibid
6 http://www.genderlinks.org.za/gelections/pressrelease.asp (accessed: 20/01/05).
7 Under the apartheid regime the population of South Africa has been divided into different race groups – White, Indian, Coloured and African – that were differently disadvantaged. Government, in all its manipulations remained White until the first democratic election in 1994.
8 Albertyn C., 1996.
9 During the mock parliaments, women and the girl-child often approach political and economic concerns through a gender lens. Mock parliaments also act as a learning tool for understanding how parliament and legislative processes work.
10 South Africa Millennium Development Goals Report, 2005.
11 Statistics South Africa, Labour Force Survey Key Findings, 2001. Available at www.statissa.gov.za/keyindicators
12 Commission on Gender Equality, Gender and the Private Sector, Johannesburg, 1999.
13 V. Robinson, "It's Sink or Swim for Sangoco", Mail and Guardian, February 2003, p21-27.
14 Statistics South Africa, Population Census, Pretoria, 1998.
15 Excluding the self-employed.
16 Statistics South Africa, Survey of the Employed and Self-Employed, 2001.
17 Ibid, in Graph 9
18 Ibid, in Graph 10
19 The narrative from the establishment of "Women's Development Bank" has testimonials from women, which refer to hostile (even racist) bank personnel, having to travel long distances to banks; being intimidated sometimes because of illiteracy, and having no access to sanitation facilities once in towns.
20 Statistics South Africa, Survey of the Employed and Self-Employed (SESE), 2001.
21 Women's Dialogue (July 2003) and Ingxoxo Zama Khosikazi (Conversations amongst Women), August 2003.
22 The Reconstruction and Development Programme, 1994 p95, paragraph4.4.7.8
23 Statistics South Africa, A Survey of Time Use – How South African Women and Men Spend their Time, Pretoria 2001 p3.
24 Lindiwe Hendricks, then Deputy Minister of Trade and Industry, 2004.
25 Ibid
26 "Gender neutral and blind" in Gender Education and Training Network Newsletter, April 2005.
27 "South Africa: Strong Rand Hurts Manufacturing Sector", Available at www.irin-news.org.report.asp.
28 Indicator, South Africa clothing, and textile assessment.V18No.4 December 2001, Available at www.ukzn.ac.za/indicator/volm18No4/18.4-fature.htm accessed on 14/6/2005.
29 Ibid
30 Daily News, 3 May 2005.
31 Saku Buhlungu and Eddie Webster "Work restructuring and the future of labour in South Africa' in Saku Buhlungu et al (eds.) State of the Nation 2005-2006 (2006) HRRC Press p248, 250.
32 Statistics South Africa, 2000, Census in Brief, 57.
33 http://www.sadcreview.com/country_profiles/southafrica/rsa_agriculture.htm, accessed on 4th October, 2005.
34 AIDC, "Food security in South Africa: the case of subsistence fisheries" Available online at http://www.sarpn.org/documents/IFSS.pdf.
35 FAO, Food and Agricultural Indicators, Country: South Africa, Available at http://www.fao.org/country profiles/index.asp accessed 16/6/2005.
36 Centre for Applied Legal Studies African Gender and Development Index, Draft Report (2005) p181.
37 Ibid
38 Statistics South Africa, Census in Brief (2003) p9.
39 J. May, I. Woolard and S. Klasen 'The nature and measurement of poverty and inequality" in May (ed.) Poverty and Inequality in South Africa: Meeting the Challenge (2000) Cape Town: David Philip.
40 Ibid, p234
41 Department of Land and Agriculture, Discussion Document on Agricultural Policy in South Africa, 1998 p10.
42 (Department of Land and Agriculture, 1998, p42).
43 Centre for Applied Legal Studies African Gender and Development Index, Draft Report (2005) p182.
44 Centre for Applied Legal Studies African Gender and Development Index, Draft Report (2005) p181.
45 Statistics South Africa Labour Force Survey, 2001.
46 Shamim Meer, 1997.
47 Walker, 2005
48 Ibid
49 Ibid
50 Ibid
51 Sanders, Nash and Hoffman, Women and Health, Maskew Miller, Cape Town, 1994 p151
52 Government of South Africa, Integrated National Disability White Paper, 1997.
53 Statistics South Africa, Figures from Census 1995 and 2001.
54 Statistics South Africa, October Household Surveys, 1995 and 1999.
55 Statistics South Africa, Women and Men in South Africa: Five Years On, Pretoria 2002.
56 Statistics South Africa, Labour Force Survey, 2003.
57 Ibid
58 Ibid
59 Piyushi Kotecha, The Position of Women Teachers, in Lessing, Margaret (ed.), South

African Women Today. Maskew Miller, Cape Town, 1994 p31.

60   Wolpe, et al, 1997.
61   Howie and Tauchert, 2002.
62   Department of Education, Education in South Africa: Achievements since 1994, Pretoria, 2001 p32.
63   Statistics South Africa, Labour Force Survey, 2002.
64   Ibid
65   Beyond Inequalities: Women in South Africa, 1997, p34
66   Statistics South Africa, Census Report 2001.
67   Ibid
68   Ibid
69   Ibid
70   2002 (1) BCLR 1 (CC).
71   Daniels v Campbell NO 2004 (7) BCLR 735 (CC).
72   Maharaj A., Virginity Testing: A matter of Abuse or Prevention? N0. 41, Agenda, 1999.
73   Commission for Gender Equality, Virginity Testing Conference Report (2003).
74   Centre for Applied Legal Studies African Gender and Development Index, Draft Report 2005 p64.
75   The Promotion of Equality and Prevention of Unfair Discrimination, Section 8(b).
76   The Promotion of Equality and Prevention of Unfair Discrimination, Section Section 8(a).
77   The Promotion of Equality and Prevention of Unfair Discrimination, Section Section 8(d).
78   Julian May (ed.), Poverty and Inequality in South Africa: Meeting the Challenge, David Philip, Cape Town, 2000.
79   Statistics South Africa, Census Report 2001.
80   WfW Annual Report 2001/02.
81   The Presidency, Towards a Ten Year Review: Synthesis Report on Implementation of Government Programmes, 2003.
82   United Nations Report Highlights Growing Inequality in South Africa, 2004.
83   The Presidency, Towards a Ten-Year Review: Synthesis Report on Implementation of Government Programmes, 2003.
84   National Population Unit, The State of South Africa's Population Report, Department of Social Development, Pretoria 2000 p46.
85   Ibid p11
86   Statistics South Africa, October Household Survey, 1995.
87   As extracted from the Draft Report of The African Gender and Development Index: South Africa's Report, 2003/2004 (Researchers: Centre for Applied Legal Studies, Witwatersrand University).
88   Department of Health, South African Demographic and Health Survey, 1998.
89   Department of Health, Saving Mothers Report on Confidential Enquiries into Maternal Deaths, 1998.
90   As reported in the Draft Report of the African Gender and Development Index: South Africa's Report, 2003/2004 (Researchers: Centre for Applied Legal Studies, Witwatersrand University).
91   Subsequent reports such as The Interim Report on Confidential Enquiry into Maternal Deaths in South Africa: March 1998; Saving Mothers – Report on Confidential Enquiries into Maternal Deaths in South Africa: 1998; The Second Interim Report on Confidential Enquiries into Maternal Deaths in SA: 1999; and Maternal Health Progress Report on Ten Points Operational Plans: 2000-2001, form the basis for informed policy formulation on maternal mortality.
92   As stated in the Draft Report of the African

Gender and Development Index: South Africa's Report, 2003/2004 (researchers: Centre for Applied Legal Studies, Witwatersrand University).
93   The total fertility rate and age specific fertility rates are a common measure of recent fertility. The total fertility rate is defined as the number of children a woman would have by the end of her child-bearing years if she were to pass through these years bearing children at the prevailing age-specific rates.
94   Women having no education have a fertility rate of 4.5; women with schooling up to Standard 3 have a fertility rate of 3.9; women with schooling between Standard 4-Standard 5 have a fertility rate of 2.5; women with schooling levels of Standard 6-Standard 9 have a fertility rate of 2.7; women with a Standard 10 education have a fertility rate of 2.2; and women who have an education level higher than Standard 10 have a fertility rate of 1.9.
95   Department of Health, South African Demographic and Health Survey, 1998.
96   Ibid
97   Ibid
98   Ibid
99   Ibid
100 Ibid
101 Ibid
102 Ibid
103 Ibid
104 Ibid
105 Ibid
106 The results of the 2002 survey have not yet been released.
107 Dunkle, Jewkes, Brown, McIntyre, Gray & Harlow, Gender-Based Violence and HIV Infection among Pregnant Women in Soweto: A Technical Report to the Australian Agency for International Development (2003) p2-3.
108 Treatment Action Campaign v Minister of Health 2002 (5) SA 721 (CC).
109 Aids Law Project, Missing the Target: A Report on HIV/AIDS Treatment Access from the Frontlines.
110 Department of Social Development, Strategic Plan 2002/3 – 2004/5 (2002).
111 C. Hardy, A. Meerkotter & M. Richter, Choosing Anti-retrovirals or Choosing Grants, Paper for the CROP CICLASS Workshop on Poverty and the Law, University of Johannesburg, January 2005, See also F. Zuberi "Hey Miss AIDS When are You Going to Receive Your Social Grant?' The Rights of Access to Social Assistance: HIV/AIDS and Disability Grants" in F. Viljoen (ed.) Fighting Stigma (2005) AIDS and Human Rights Research Unit, University of Pretoria.
112 Viljoen F., (ed.) Fighting Stigma (2005) AIDS and Human Rights Research Unit, University of Pretoria.
113 S., Leclerc Madlala 'Virginity testing: Managing Sexuality in a Maturing HIV/AIDS Epidemic', Medical Anthropology Quarterly, (2001) p15.
114 As extracted from the Draft Report of the African Gender and Development Index: South African Section, 2003/2004 (Researchers: Centre for Applied Legal Studies, Witwatersrand University).
115 Tamara Braam, 1999.
116 South African Police Service.
117 Vetten & Bhana, Violence, Vengeance and Gender: A Preliminary Investigation into the Links Between Violence against Women and HIV/AIDS in South Africa (2001).
118 Park, Fedler & Dangor (eds.) Reclaiming Women's Spaces (2000) p51. For a discussion of the various studies and sources estimating prevalence see Rasool, Vermaak, Pharaoh, Louw

& Stavrou Violence Against Women: A National Survey (2000) p8 and Ludsin & Vetten Spiral of Entrapment (2005) p9.
119 See, inter alia, Vetten, "Gender, Race and Power Dynamics" in Park, Fedler & Dangor (eds.) Reclaiming Women's Spaces: New Perspectives on Violence against Women and Sheltering in South Africa (2000) p57; Mathews & Abrahams, Combining Stories and Numbers: An Analysis of the Impact of the Domestic Violence Act (No. 116 of 1998) on Women (2001) p9.
120 Results of a National Youth Survey.
121 Vetten & Bhana, Violence, Vengeance and Gender: A Preliminary Investigation into the Links Between Violence against Women and HIV/AIDS in South Africa (2001). See also Albertyn (2001) Law, Democracy and Development.
122 Dunkle, Jewkes, Brown, McIntyre, Gray & Harlow, Gender-Based Violence and HIV Infection among Pregnant Women in Soweto: A Technical Report to the Australian Agency for International Development (2003) p2-3.
123 Everatt, "Findings of the CASE Study: Excerpts from Where are the Women? Analysing the Representation of Women in the Media," 1997.
124 Women's Media Watch, "A Snapshot Survey of Women's Representation in the South African Media at the end of the Millennium," 1999.
125 Ibid
126 Gender Links and MISA, The Southern African Gender and Media Baseline Study, 2002.
127 Commission on Gender Equality, "Media Coverage of Women During the 1999 Elections", 1999b.
128 Everatt, "Findings of the CASE study: Excerpts from Where are the Women? Analysing the Representation of Women in the Media," 1997.
129 Gender Links and MISA, The Southern African Gender and Media Baseline Study, 2002.
130 Gender Advocacy Project, "Women in Government: 50/50 by 2005," 2002. Gender Links, "Number of Women in Parliament up by Ten Percent," 2004.
131 Commission on Gender Equality, "Media Coverage of Women during the 1999 Elections" 1999b.
132 Bird W., "Monitoring Gender and the Elections – 29th April 2004," 2004.
133 Gender Links, "Number of Women in Parliament up by ten percent," 2004.
134 Commission on Gender equality, "Gender and Media Directory 1999-2000," 1999a.
135 Media Monitoring Project, "Gender, Politics and Media: Summary of Research by the Media Monitoring Project," May 1999.
136 Garda and Bird, "Reporting Abortion: An Analysis of Media Coverage of the Choice of Termination of Pregnancy Act," 1997.
137 Ziyambi N.M., "Women's Groups and the Media in Zimbabwe: Strategies for Access and Participation," 1997.
138 Gender Links and MISA, The Southern African Gender and Media Baseline Study, 2002; SANEF, "2002 South African National Journalism Skills Audit," 2002.
139 SANEF, "2002 South African National Journalism Skills Audit," 2002.
140 Gender Links and MISA, The Southern African Gender and Media Baseline Study, 2002.
141 Ibid
142 SANEF, "2002 South African National Journalism Skills Audit," 2002.
143 Sapa, "Women's Story Untold," 2000.
144 Ziyambi, Women's Groups and the Media in Zimbabwe: Strategies for Access and Participation, 1997.
145 Smith, "Women Working on the Internet: New Frontiers for Exclusion?" 1998.
146 Lowe, Morna, "Empowerment Through ICTs with Special Reference to African Media Women 2001," 2001.
147 Smith, "Women Working on the Internet: New Frontiers for Exclusion?" 1998.
148 This section draws considerably from the draft report of the African Gender and Development Index, Centre for Applied Legal Studies Draft Report (2005) Chapter one.
149 The Constitution for the Republic of South Africa, Section 1.
150 Ibid, Section 9. This right includes provision for protection against unfair discrimination, as well as provision for remedial positive measures to achieve equality.
151 Ibid, Section 12.
152 Ibid, Section 16(2)(c).
153 These include justiciable rights of access to adequate housing (s 26), rights of access to healthcare services, including reproductive healthcare, sufficient food and water and social security, (s 27). These are subject to progressive realisation. See Grootboom vThe Government of the Republic of South Africa 2001 (1) SA 46 (CC) for an example of how these rights have been made justiciable by the South African courts. Also at www.concourt.gov.za.
154 Section 187(1) of the 1996 Constitution requires the Commission on Gender Equality 'must promote respect for gender equality and the protection, development and attainment of gender equality.'
155 The Office on the Status of Women South Africa's National Policy Framework for Women's Empowerment and Gender Equality (2000).
156 Commission for Gender Equality, A Framework for Transforming Gender Relations (1999) Draft 4.
157 This section draws considerably from the report of the African Gender and Development Index, Centre for Applied Legal Studies Draft Report (2005) Chapter one.
158 South Africa Yearbook 2002/2003 (2003) p52.
159 Bell, et al, "National Machineries for Women in Development: Experiences, Lessons and Strategies" BRIDGE, Report No. 66. 2002 p3.
160 The Office on the Status of Women, South Africa's National Policy Framework for Women's Empowerment and Gender Equality (2000) para 4.4.2.
161 Ibid, paragraph 4.5. See para 4.6 for proposed gender structures in local government.
162 Ibid, paragraph 4.4.3.
163 Ibid, paragraph 4.4.4.
164 Office on the Status of Women, Status of Gender Focal Points in National Departments Audit Report (2002).
165 Ibid
166 The Office on the Status of Women, South Africa's National Policy Framework for Women's Empowerment and Gender Equality (2000) Para 4.2.3.
167 This analysis draws considerably from the report of the African Gender and Development Index,Centre for Applied Legal Studies Draft Report (2005) Chapter one.
168 Ibid
169 There are 36 national departments in South Africa, of which 29 responded to the 2003 Audit.
170 Even though 15 departments reported that their GFP functions are reflected in their performance agreements, a further analysis showed that children's rights, disability, and HIV and AIDS are also within their performance contracts.
171 The departments have varying organograms. However, broadly speaking, a

Director has the following positions in the unit: Deputy Director/s; Assistant Director/s; and Administrative staff.

172 A thorough analysis would enable government to review both systems in place (internal transformation) and the impact of government programmes (external transformation) from a gendered analysis.

173 This issue was raised by women delegates to the Ingxoxo Zamakhosikazi (Conversations among Women) held on 26-27 August 2003 as a matter of concern, and as an issue which needs to be addressed.

174 During the mock parliaments, women and the girl-child often approach political and economic concerns through a gender lens. Mock parliaments also act as a learning tool for understanding how parliament and legislative processes work.

175 Labour Relations Act 66 , 1997.

176 Employment Equity User Guide, 1999.

177 The programmes and policies as highlighted in the speech delivered by the Deputy Minister for Trade and Industry to the National Assembly, in the national debate on "Quality of Life and Status of Women in South Africa" on 03 September 2003.

178 Government of South Africa, Towards a Ten-Year Review, Synthesis and Implementation Report, 2004.

179 The take-up rates of the child support grant increased in the 2001/2002 financial year to around 1.5 million out of, at the very least, 3 million eligible children.

180 Ibid

181 Statistics South Africa, Labour Force Survey, September 2002, (Reliable Figures are only available at the household level).

182 Sex disaggregated data indicating how women and the girl-child have benefited from the different types of grants was not readily available at the time of compiling this report. Whilst Annexure 4 of this report provides a comprehensive breakdown of the beneficiaries as per individual grant types for the period April 2000 to February 2003, this data is not disaggregated according to sex.

183 The number of foster care grants has increased by 85,577 between April 2000 and February 2003. The increase in Limpopo Province (7,964) and Kwa-Zulu Natal (22,776) account for most of this increase. However, the data provided does not indicate a disaggregation according to sex. (As reported in the Press Briefing Memorandum, issued by the Minister of Social Development entitled "Fact Sheet: Social Grants Beneficiaries".)

184 Transforming the Present – Protecting the Future: Consolidated Report of the Committee of Enquiry into a Comprehensive System of Social Security for South Africa, March 2002, p79.

185 As identified by women delegates to the "Conversations Amongst Women" held on 26-27 August 2003.

186 Transforming the Present – Protecting the Future: Consolidated Report of the Committee of Inquiry into a Comprehensive System of Social Security for South Africa; March 2002, p80-81.

187 Figures sourced from "Towards Ten Years of Freedom", South African Government, p85

188 Ibid

189 Letter from Mrs Z. Mbeki dated 23 October 2001.

190 These Programmes are put in place by the national Department for Housing to address the inequalities in home ownership experienced as a result of race and gender discrimination of the past.

191 Statistics South Africa, 2003.

192 As stated in "Overview: Social Sector", a report prepared by the Chief Directorate, Social Sector, PCAS, The Presidency, 2003.

193 Currently a draft document produced by the Department of Land Affairs.

194 Department of Land Affairs White Paper on Land Reform (1997).

195 Ibid, 15

196 Department of Land Affairs Land Reform Gender Policy- A Framework (1997) p2-3.

197 Walker, "'Piety in the Sky?' Gender Programmes and Land Reform in South Africa" (2003) 3(1) & (2) Journal of Agrarian Change, p113.

198 Agriculture and Land Affairs Policy Statement by Minister for Agriculture and Land Affairs for Strategic Direction on Land Issues (2000).

199 Cross & D., Hornby, (2005) Opposition and Obstacles to Women's Land Access in South Africa: Past, Present and Future (2002) National Land Committee and Department of Land Affairs, p140.

200 According to data provided in the Department of Land Affairs' Statistical Report compiled by the Department's Monitoring and Evaluation Directorate.

201 Walker. C, Women "Gender Relations and Land Rights in South Africa" (2005) Politikon.

202 As extracted from the Draft Report of the African Gender and Development Index: South Africa's Report, 2003/2004 (Researchers: Centre for Applied Legal Studies, Witwatersrand University).

203 Termination of Pregnancy Act, 1996.

204 As reported in the Draft Report of the African Gender and Development Index: South Africa's Report, 2003/2004.

205 National Population Unit, the State of South Africa's Population Report 2000, Department of Social Development Pretoria 2000, p58.

206 Department of Health, 2000.

207 Muthien B., Strategic Interventions: Intersections Between Gender-Based Violence and HIV/AIDS, Gender Project, Community Law Centre, University of the Western Cape, Cape Town, 2003.

208 Human Rights Watch, Scared at School: Sexual Violence against Girls in South Africa, Human Rights Watch, New York, 2001.

209 Draft Report of the African Gender and Development Index: South Africa's Report, 2003/2004 (Researchers: Centre for Applied Legal Studies, Witwatersrand University).

210 Draft Report of the African Gender and Development Index: South African Section which quoted the source as CIET Africa "A Culture of Sexual Violence" www.ciet.org.za

211 These would be cases that do not involve an employer/employee relationship.

212 The South African Country Report and the Report of the National Stakeholders' Consultative Conference held during February 2003 in preparation for the 47th Session of the UN CSW.

213 Issue Paper 19, Project 107, 12 July 2002.

214 Babalo,Ndenze. http://www.sauvca.org.za_new/326904.htm (accessed 20/01/05).

215 Gender Unit, Department of Science and Technology, 2003.

216 Gender Unit, Department of Science and Technology, 2004.

BIBLIOGRAPHY

ADRA, Development Workshop and SARDC WIDSAA, *Beyond Inequalities: Women in Angola*, ADRA/DW/SARDC, Luanda and Harare, 2000.

AIDS Law Project, Missing the Target, A Report on HIV/AIDS Treatment Access from the front lines, Johannesburg, 2006

Albertyn, C., "IDASA/LOGIC Women in Local Government: Breaking Barriers Conference, Plenary Speeches", 17-18 June 1996, Cape Town, 1996.

Barbeton, C., Blake, M., and Kotzé, H., (eds.), *Creating Action Space: the Challenge of Poverty and Democracy in South Africa*, IDASA, Cape Town, 1998.

Bell, E., et al., *National Machineries for Women in Development: Experiences, Lessons and Strategies*, BRIDGE, Report No. 66, 2002.

Beyond Inequalities: Women in Southern Africa 2005 series for Botswana, Malawi, Mozambique, Namibia, South Africa, Zambia, Zimbabwe published by SARDC and partners, 2005/6
Beyond Inequalities: Women in Southern Africa, plus individual titles for 12 SADC countries, published by SARDC and partners 1997-2000

Bird, W., Monitoring *Gender and the Elections – 29th April 2004,* http://www.sn.apc.org/mmp.

Boyle, B., "Manuel Calls for Jobs not Handouts: Social Spending", in *Business Times,* 5 September 2004.

Braam, T., *Making the Link between Violence against Women and Health, Connection,* Vol. 3 No. 2, Reproductive Rights Alliance, Johannesburg, July 1999.

Bond, P. and Khosa, M., (eds.), *An RDP Policy Audit,* ANC, P & DM Wits, HSRC, Pretoria, 1999.

Bradshaw, D. and Steyn, K., *Poverty and Chronic Diseases in South Africa, Technical Report,* Medical Research Council, Pretoria, 2001.

Budlender, D., *Women and Men in South Africa,* Central Statistical Service, Pretoria, 1998.
_____*The Women's Budget,* IDASA, Cape Town, 1998.
_____ The *Fourth Women's Budget,* IDASA, Cape Town, 1999a.
_____ *Participation of Women in the Legislative Process,* The European Parliamentary Support Programme, Cape Town, 1999b.

Centre for African Studies, Eduardo Mondlane University, Forum Mulher and SARDC WIDSAA, *Beyond Inequalities: Women in Mozambique,* CEA/FM/SARDC, Maputo and Harare, 2000.
Centre for Applied Legal Studies, *Handbook on National and Provincial Machinery for Advancing Gender Equality,* Centre for Applied Legal Studies (University of the Witwatersrand) and the Commonwealth Secretariat, Johannesburg, 1996.
Centre for Applied Legal Studies, *African Gender and Development Index - The African Gender and Development Index: South Africa's Report 2003/2004,* Centre for Applied Legal Studies, Witwatersrand University, 2003.

Christofedes, N., et al., *The State of Sexual Assault Services: Findings from a Situation Analysis of Services in South Africa,* The South African Gender-based Violence and Health Initiative, Medical Research Council, Pretoria, 2003.

Commission on Gender Equality, *A Framework for Transforming Gender Relations in South Africa,* CGE, Johannesburg, 2000.
Commission on Gender Equality, *A Gender Analysis of the Maputo Development Corridor,* CGE, Braamfontein, 1999.
Commission on Gender Equality, Gender *Opinion Survey,* CGE, Johannesburg, 2001.
Commission on Gender Equality, Gender *and the Private Sector,* CGE, Johannesburg, 1999.
Commission on Gender Equality, Gender *and Media Directory 1999-2000,* CGE, Johannesburg, 2000.
Commission on Gender Equality, (Media Coverage of Women During the 1999 elections.) *Review of the 1999 General Elections – a Gender Perspective,* CGE, Braamfontein, 2000.
Commission on Gender Equality, "Report of the Commission on Gender Equality Information and Evaluation Workshops", CGE, Pretoria, 1997.

Community Workers Co-operative, "Women in South Africa: Challenges for Collective Action in the New Millennium", Community Workers Co-operative, Ireland, 2003.

Cross, C., *Women and Land in the Rural Crisis, Agenda* Vol 14 No 2, Land Research Action Network, New York, 1999.

Daniel, J., Habib, A., and Southall, R., *State of the Nation South Africa 2003 –2004,* HSRC, Pretoria, 2003.

Delport, E., *The State of Gender Mainstreaming in South Africa,* University of Pretoria, Pretoria, 2000.

Department of Education, *Annual Report, DOE,* Pretoria, 2002.
Department of Education, *Education in South Africa: Achievements since 1994,* DOE, Pretoria, 2001.
Department of Education, *Gender, Development and Planning Training Programme* Department of Education, Available at www.doe.gov.za.
Department of Education, *Education White Paper 3: A Programme for the Transformation of Higher Education,* DOE, Pretoria, 1997.
Department of Health, *HIV/AIDS/STD: Strategic Plan for South Africa 2000-2005,* Department of Health, Pretoria, 2000.
Department of Health, *Saving Mothers: Report on Confidential Inquiries into Maternal Deaths in South Africa 1998,* Government Printer, Pretoria, 1999.
Department of Health, *White Paper for the Transformation of the Health System in South Africa,*

Government Gazette No. 17910, Ministry of Health, Durban, 1997.
Department of Justice, *Gender Policy, Department* of Justice, Pretoria, 1997.
Department of Labour, *Commission for Employment Equity: Annual Report 2001 – 2002,* DOL, Pretoria, 2003.
Department of Labour, *National Skills Development Strategy,* DOL, Pretoria, 2001.
Department of Labour, *Towards a National   Labour Action Programme for South Africa,* DOL, Pretoria, 2002.
Department of Labour – Government of South Africa, Labour Related Laws: Skills Development Act 97 of 1998: Adult Basic Education and Training Act 52 of 2000: South African Qualifications Authority Act 58 of 1995: National Skills Development Strategy.
Department of Social Development, "Report of the Committee of Inquiry into a Comprehensive System of Social Security for South Africa", Dept. of Social Development, Pretoria, 2002.
Department of Social Development, "The State of South Africa's Population Report 2000", National Population Unit, Pretoria, 2000.
Department of Water Affairs and Forestry, Gender Policy 2002 – 2003, Department of Water Affairs and Forestry, Pretoria, 2003.

Ditshwanelo and SARDC WIDSAA, *Beyond Inequalities: Women in Botswana*, Ditshwanelo /SARDC, Gaborone and Harare, 1998.

Edigheji, S., "Casualisation of the Teacher", Agenda, No 41, University of KwaZulu-Natal, Durban, 1999.

FAO, "Food and Agricultural Indicators. Country: South Africa", Available at www.fao.org/country profiles/index. asp

Fick, G., Gender Checklist for Free and Fair Elections: A Handbook, Electoral Institute of South Africa, Johannesburg, 1999.

Fok, Lauren, Letter to the Editors: Rebuttal, 2004. Available at
www.womensnet.org.za/elections2004/idex

Gap Talk, "Legislate a Gender Quota within the PR System", Gap Talk No 10, GAP, Cape Town, 2002.
Gap Talk, "Electoral Systems and Women's Inclusion: Local Government and Gender", Gap Talk No. 10, GAP, Cape Town, 2002.

Garda, Z. and Bird, E., "Reporting Abortion: An Analysis of Media Coverage of the Choice of Termination of Pregnancy Act", Report of the Gender in Media Symposium held in Johannesburg, September 26 1997, CGE, Johannesburg, 1997.

Gender Advocacy Programme, "Concerns around the Child Support Grant in Social Policy", GAP, Cape Town, 2001.
Gender Advocacy Programme, "Gender and Performance Indicators for Local Government", GAP, Cape Town, 2002.
Gender Advocacy Programme, "Mainstreaming Gender in Government: The Role of Civil Society", GAP, Cape Town, 2000.
Gender Advocacy Project, "Women in Government: 50/50 by 2005", GAP, Cape Town, 2002.
Gender Advocacy Programme, "Women and Local Government" GAP, No. 3, Cape Town, 1997/8.

Gender Links, Case Study on Radio Islam, South Africa, 2001.
www.genderlinks.org.za/docs/2001/radioislam-casestudy.pdf
Gender Links, "Number of Women in Parliament up by Ten Percent", Gender Links, 2004.
Gender Links and Media Institute of Southern Africa, the Southern African Gender and Media Baseline Study: South Africa, 2003.
www.genderlinks.org.za/policyresearch/gmbaseline.htm.

Gouws, A., "Floor-crossing and Participatory Democracy", Gap Talk No. 10, GAP, Cape Town, 2002.

Govender, P., (Ed.), "Beijing Conference Report: 1994 Country Report on the Status of South African Women", Government of South Africa, Pretoria, 1994.

Government of South Africa, *Constitution of the Republic of South Africa,* Government Printer, Pretoria, 1996.
Government of South Africa, "Poverty and Inequality in South Africa: Report prepared for the Office of the Executive Deputy President and the Ministerial Committee for Poverty and Inequality", Government Printer, Pretoria, 1998.
Government of South Africa, White Paper on the Transformation of the Public Sector, 1995, Government Printer, Pretoria,   1995.
Government of South Africa, South Africa Yearbook 2000/1, Government Printer, Pretoria, 2001.
Government of South Africa, South Africa Yearbook. 2003/4, Government Printer, Pretoria, 2004.
Government of South Africa, South Africa National Report on Social Development 1995-2000, Government Printer, Pretoria, 1995.
Government of South Africa, "Towards a Ten Year Review: Synthesis Report on Implementation of Government Programmes: Discussion document", The Presidency, Pretoria, 2003.
Government of South Africa, Integrated National Disability White paper, Government Printers, Pretoria, 1997.
Government of the Republic of South Africa, Choice on the Termination of Pregnancy Act of 1996, Government Printer, Pretoria, 1996.

Gray, M.M., and Sathiparsad, R., "Violence Against Women in South Africa: An Analysis of Media Coverage", Vol 34, No.3, University of KwaZulu-Natal, Department of Social Work, Durban, 1998.

Green, P., "An Absence of Women: At Newspapers in South Africa Few Women are at the Top, Some Wonder Why and Ask Why it Matters", in Nieman Reports, New York, 2001.

Hall, R., Jacobs, P. and Lahiff, E., Evaluating Land and Agrarian Reform in South Africa, An Occassional Paper Series, No. 10, Final Report, PLAAS, University of the Western Cape, Bellville, 2003.

Hames, M., The Appointment of Women in Senior Management Positions at the Universities of the Western Cape and Stellenbosch: A Study of the Implementation of Equity Legislation, 1999-2002, University of Port Elizabeth, Port Elizabeth, 2003. (Unpublished M Phil Thesis).

Hardy, C., Meerkotter, A., and Richter, M., Choosing Anti-retrovirals or Choosing Grants Paper for the CROP CICLASS Workshop on Poverty and the Law, University of Johannesburg, Johannesburg, 2005.

Health Systems Trust, South African Health Review 2001, Health Systems Trust, Durban, 2002.

Henry, J. Kaiser Family Foundation, Impending Catastrophe Revisited: An Update on the HIV/AIDS Epidemic in South Africa, Henry J. Kaiser Foundation, Johannesburg, 1996.

Hirschowitz, R. and Orkin, M., A National Household Survey of Health Inequalities in South Africa: An Overview Report, Henry J. Kaiser Family Foundation, Washington, 1995.

Houston, A., Women and Local Government: A Study into the Expectations Women have on Local Government, GAP, Cape Town, 1996.

Howie, G. and Tauchert, A., (Eds), Gender, Teaching and Research in Higher Education: Challenges for the 21st Century, Ashgate Publishing, Hampshire, 2002.

Human Rights Watch, Scared at School Sexual Harassment in South African Schools, HRW, New York, 2001.

Independent Broadcasting Authority, "Position Paper on the Revision of the IBA's Code of Conduct for Broadcasters", IBA, Johannesburg, 1999.

Institute of Race Relations, South Africa Survey 2002/3, SAIIR, Johannesburg, 2003.

International Organisation of Migration, Trafficking in Women and Children for Sexual Exploitation in Southern Africa, International Organisation of Migration, Pretoria , 2003.

Jewkes, R., Abuse of Trust: Teachers Raping School Girls, WHP Review No. 41, WHP, Johannesburg, 2002.
Jewkes, R., et al., "Developing an Appropriate Health Sector Response to Gender-based Violence", SA Gender Based Violence and Health Initiative Workshop report, Medical Research Council, Pretoria, 2001.

Kallmann, K., HIV/AIDS and Social Assistance in South Africa, South African Legal Assistance Network/Black Sash Trust, 2003.

Kehler, J., Rights and Realities: A Handbook of Women's Rights in South Africa, National Association of Democratic Lawyers; Human Rights Research and Advocacy Project, Cape Town, 2000.

Kenyon, C., Heywood, M. and Conway, S., Mainstreaming HIV/AIDS: Progress and Challenges: South African Health Review 2001, Health Systems Trust, Durban, 2002.

Kepe, T. and Cousins, B., (2002), "Radical Land Reform is the Key to Sustainable Rural Development in South Africa", Policy in Brief: Debating Land Reform and Rural Development: No. 3 August, University of the Western Cape, PLAAS, Bellville, 2002.

Klugman, B. and Moornman, J., Gender and the Empowerment Issues within the Health Sector, WHP Review, No. 44, Johannesburg, 2003.

Knight, R., "A Decade of Democracy: Housing, Services and Land in South Africa", South Africa Delegation Briefing Paper, April 22-May 2, 2004.
www.richardknight.homestead.com/files/sihousing2004.htm

Koen, K. and Van Vuuren, B., Children in Domestic Service: The Case of the Western Cape, terre des hommes, Switzerland, 2002.

Lahiff, E., Land Reform in South Africa: Is it Meeting the Challenge? Policy in Brief: Debating Land Reform and Rural Development, No. 1 September, PLAAS University of the Western Cape, Bellville, 2001.

Leclerc Madlala S., "Virginity Testing: Managing Sexuality in a Maturing HIV/AIDS Epidemic", in Medical Anthropology Quarterly, New York, 2001.

Lowe-Morna, C., "Empowerment Through ICTs with Special Reference to African Media Women 2001", Paper Presented at Inception of the East African Media Women's Association website, Nairobi, March 2001,www.genderlinks.org.za/docs/2001/gendermedia-ictpresent.pdf
Lowe-Morna, C., "Ready to Rise: A Case Study of Good Practice in Establishing a Proactive Gender Policy", Presented at a Reading, Training Workshop on Gender Justice and Organisational Transformation, November (AGI & P & DM), 1998.
Lowe-Morna, C., (ed.), Ringing up the Changes: Gender in Southern African Politics, Gender Links, Johannesburg, 2004.

Magardie, K., "More than Just Brainless Sex Objects", Mail & Guardian, 2000, Available at www.sn.apc.org/wmail/issues/00331/NEWS38.html

Maharaj, A., "Provinces Quick-pick Gender Focal Points", Agenda, No. 41, Human Rights Watch, New York, 1999.
Maharaj, A., Redefining Violence against Women in the New Millennium. Connections, Vol. 3 No. 4, Human Rights Watch, New York, 1999.
Mauritius Alliance of Women and SARDC WIDSAA, *Beyond Inequalities: Women in Mauritius*, MAW/SARDC, Quatre-Bornes and Harare, 1997.

May J., Woolard, I. and Klasen, S., "The nature and measurement of poverty and inequality" in May J, (ed.) Poverty and Inequality in South Africa: Meeting the Challenge, David Phillip, Cape Town, 2000.

McCoy, D., et al., Interim Findings on the National PMTCT Pilot Sites: Lessons and Recommendations, Health Systems Trust, Durban, 2002.

Media Monitoring Project, "Gender, Politics and Media: Summary of Research by the Media

Monitoring Project", Proceedings of the National Gender and Media Symposium held by the Commission on Gender Equality, May 14 1999 at the Parktonian Hotel, Johannesburg, 1999.
Meer, S., (ed.), Women, Land and Authority: Perspectives from South Africa, David Philip, and Oxford: Oxfam, Braamfontein, National Land Commission, Cape Town, 1997.

Menell, K. and Jobson, M., Women's Rights in South Africa: A Guide to National Organisations with a Gender Focus, Institute of South Africa, HSRC, Pretoria, 1995.

Merton, R.K., and Nisbet, R., (eds.), Contemporary Social Problems, 4th ed., Harcourt Brace Jovanovich, New York, 1976.

Mjoli-Mncube, N., "Land and Housing: Women Speak Out", Agenda 42, 1999.

Mokwana, M., "Women of Moutse Capture the Airwaves", Agenda 38, 1998.

Molo Songololo, "Trafficking of Children for Purposes of Sexual Exploitation South Africa A Report", Cape Town, 2000.

Moultrie, T.A. and Timaeus, I.M., "Trends in South African Fertility Between 1970 and 1998: An Analysis of the 1996 Census and the 1998 Demographic and Health Survey, Technical Report", Medical Research Council, Burden of Disease Research Unit, Pretoria, 2002.

Moya, Fikile-Ntsikelelo, "Time to Close Chapter 9?" Mail & Guardian, June 4-10, 2004.

Muthien, B., "Strategic Interventions: Intersections Between Gender-Based Violence and HIV/AIDS", Gender Project Community Law Centre University of the Western Cape, Bellville, 2003.

Mutume, G., Rights – South Africa: Women Celebrate Gains, World News Inter Press Service, Durban, 1998.

National Population Unit, The State of South Africa's Population, Population, Poverty and Vulnerability, Department of Social Development, Pretoria, 2000.
National Sanitation Task Team, White Paper on Basic Household Sanitation, Department of Water Affairs and Forestry, Pretoria, 2001.

Ngubane, S., "Title to Land?" Agenda 42, 1999.

Nyman, R., Globalisation and the South African Economy – Does it Benefit the Working Class? ILRIG, Cape Town, 2000.

Office on the Status of Women, South Africa's National Policy Framework for Women's Empowerment and Gender Equality, OSW, Pretoria, 2000.

Parenzee, P., Artz, L. and Moult, K.., "Monitoring the Implementation of the Domestic Violence Act: First Report 2000-2001", Institute of Criminology, University of Cape Town, Cape Town, 2001.

Parliamentary Committee on the Improvement and the Quality of Life and Status of Women, Report on Governments' Implementation of CEDAW and the Beijing Platform of Action, Parliamentary Committee on the Improvement and the Quality of Life and Status of Women, Pretoria, 1998.

Petros, N., "White Males Still Top of the Job Pile – Report: Outlook for Advancing Equity Bleak", Business Day, 25 April 2003.

Pincus, J., Our Bodies, Ourselves for the New Century: A Book by and for Women, in The Boston Women's Health Book Collective, Simon & Schuster, New York, 1998.

Policy Coordination and Advisory Services, "Towards a Ten Year Review: Synthesis Report on Implementation of Government Programmes: A Discussion Document", The Presidency, Pretoria, 2003.

Primo, N., "Parliament, Offices of the President and Deputy President, South African Communications Service and Premiers' Votes", in Budlender, Debbie, The Third Women's Budget, IDASA, Cape Town, 1998.
Prinsloo, J., "Cheer the Beloved Country? Some Thoughts on Gendered Representations, Nationalism and the Media", Agenda 40, 1999.

Qeqe, P., "Political Parties Come out in Support of 50/50: Women in Governance", Gap Talk, Winter No.11, GAP, CapeTown, 2003.

Robinson, V., "In Pursuit of the Pound Seats: Gender Empowerment Still Takes a Back Seat to Black Economic Empowerment, writes Vicki Robinson", Mail & Guardian, March 12 to 18, 2004.
Robinson, V., "Scarcity of Women in Corporate Power: Only Three Women are Among the 25 Most Influential Black Directors in the Country", Mail & Guardian, March 12 to 18, 2004.
Robinson, V., "It's Sink or Swim for Sangaco", Mail & Guardian, February 2003.

SADC, SADC Gender and Development Declaration, SADC Secretariat, Gaborone, 1997.
SADC and SARDC, SADC Gender Monitor, Gaborone/Harare, 1999, 2001, 2006.

SARDC-WIDSAA, Beyond Inequalities: Women in Southern Africa, SARDC, Harare, 2000.

Sanders, H.R., Nash, E. and Hoffman, M., Women and Health, in Lessing, Margaret (ed.), South African Women Today. Maskew Miller, Cape Town, 1994.

Shevel, A., "Hospitals Offer Incentives in a Bid to Keep their Staff", in, Business Times, 2 February 2003.

Smith, G., "Women Working on the Internet: New Frontiers for Exclusion?" Agenda, 38,1998.

South Africa Institute of Race Relations, South Africa Survey 2000/01, SAIRR, Johannesburg, 2002.

Statistics South Africa, A Survey of Time Use – How South African Women and Men Spend Their Time, Statistics South Africa, Pretoria, 2001.
Statistics South Africa, Census in Brief: 2001 2nd ed. Statistics South Africa, Pretoria, 2003.
Statistics South Africa, Earning and Spending in South Africa Selected Findings and Comparisons from

the Income and Expenditure Surveys of October 1995 and October 2000, Pretoria, Statistics South Africa, Pretoria, 2002.
Statistics South Africa, Labour Force Survey, Statistics South Africa, Pretoria, 2001.
Statistics South Africa, Women and Men in South Africa: Five Years On, Statistics South Africa, Pretoria, 2002.

State of the Nation Address of the President of South Africa, Thabo Mbeki, House of Parliament, Cape Town, 14 February 2003, Available at www.info.gov.za/speeches/2003/htm

Tanzania Gender Networking Programme and SARDC WIDSAA, *Beyond Inequalities: Women in Tanzania*, TGNP/SARDC, Dar es Salaam and Harare, 1997.

TB Indaba, Newsletter of the National TB Control Programme, No. 1 March, Department of Health, Pretoria, 2003.

Thompson, K. and Woolard, I., Achieving Employment Equity in the Public Service: A Study of Changes Between 1995 and 2001, DRU Working Paper 02/61, Cape Town: University of Cape Town, Development Policy Research Unit, 2002.

UNAM and SARDC WIDSAA, *Beyond Inequalities 2005: Women in Namibia*, UNAM/ SARDC, Windhoek and Harare, 2005.

UNIMA Centre for Social Research and SARDC WIDSAA, *Beyond Inequalities: Women in Malawi*, UNIMA/ SARDC, Zomba and Harare, 1997.

United Nations Development Programme, Human Development Report, Oxford University Press, New York, 2000.
United Nations Report Highlights Growing Inequality in South Africa.
Available at www.wsws.org/articles/2004/may2004/safr-m21.shtml

University of Namibia and SARDC-WIDSAA, *Beyond Inequalities: Women in Namibia*, UNAM/ SARDC, Windhoek and Harare, 1997.

UWC Gender Equity Unit and SARDC WIDSAA, *Beyond Inequalities: Women in South Africa*, UWC/SARDC, Bellville and Harare, 1997.

Van der Vindt, R., Report on HIV/AIDS and Violence Against Women, AIDS Law Project Policy Review and Update, Cape Town, 1998.

Van Donk, M., Challenging Gender Politics at Local Level: The Local Government Elections, Conference Organised by the Gender Advocacy Programme (GAP), 31 May-2 June 2000, GAP, Cape Town, 2000.

Vetten, L., Research into Preventing Intimate Femicide in the Gauteng Province, WHP Review, No. 45, GAP, Cape Town, 2003.

Viljoen, F., (ed.), Fighting Stigma, AIDS and Human Rights Research Unit University of Pretoria, Pretoria, 2005.

Walker, C., Land Reform and Gender in Post-apartheid South Africa: Discussion paper, United Nations Research Institute for Social Development, Geneva, 1998.

Wasserman, H. and Jacobs, S., (eds.), Post-apartheid Essays on Mass Media, Culture and Identity, Kwela Books, Cape Town, 2003.

Webster, N., Braam, T. and Matoane, T., Making the Link Between Violence Against Women and Development: Connections, Vol. 3, 1999.

WLSA Lesotho and SARDC WIDSAA, *Beyond Inequalities: Women in Lesotho*, WLSA/SARDC, Maseru and Harare, 1997.
WLSA Malawi and SARDC WIDSAA, *Beyond Inequalities 2005: Women in Malawi*, WLSA/ SARDC, Limbe and Harare, 2005.
WLSA Swaziland and SARDC WIDSAA, *Beyond Inequalities: Women in Swaziland*, WLSA/SARDC, Mbabane and Harare, 1998.

Wolpe, A., Quinlan, O. and Martinez, L., "Gender Equity in Education: A Report by the Gender Equity Task Team", Department of Education, Pretoria, 1997.

Women's Media Watch (SA), "A Snapshot Survey of Women's Representation in the South African Media at the End of the Millennium", Conducted by the Media Monitoring Project, Commissioned by Women's Media Watch (SA), Cape Town, December 1999.
Women's NGO Coalition and SARDC WIDSAA, *Beyond Inequalities 2005: Women in Botswana*, WNGOC/SARDC, Gaborone and Harare, 2005.

Zambia Association for Research and Development and SARDC, *Beyond Inequalities: Women in Zambia*, Lusaka and Harare, 1998.

ZARD and SARDC, *Beyond Inequalities 2005: Women in Zambia*, Lusaka and Harare, 2005.

Zimbabwe Women' Resource Centre and Network and SARDC WIDSAA, *Beyond Inequalities: Women in Zimbabwe*, ZWRCN/ SARDC, Harare, 1998.

Ziyambi, N. M., "Women's Groups and the Media in Zimbabwe: Strategies for Access and Participation: Women's Action Group and the Federation of African Media Women-Zimbabwe", Department of Media and Communication, University of Oslo, Oslo, 1997.

ZWRCN and SARDC WIDSAA, *Beyond Inequalities 2005: Women in Zimbabwe*, ZWRCN/ SARDC, Harare, 2005.

APPENDIX 1

GENDER AND DEVELOPMENT

A Declaration by Heads of State or Government of the Southern African Development Community (SADC)

PREAMBLE

WE, the Heads of State or Government of the Southern African Development Community,

A.   NOTING THAT:

i)   Member States undertook in the SADC Treaty and in the Declaration to the Treaty, and in the Protocol on Immunities and Privileges, SADC not to discriminate against any person on the grounds of gender, among others;

ii)   All SADC member states have signed and ratified or acceded to the UN Convention on the Elimination of All Forms of Discrimination Against Women (CEDAW), or are in the final stages of doing so.

B.   CONVINCED THAT:

i)   Gender equality is a fundamental human right;

ii)   Gender is an area in which considerable agreement already exists and where there are substantial benefits to be gained from closer regional co-operation and collective action;

iii)   The integration and mainstreaming of gender issues into the SADC Programme of Action and Community Building Initiative is key to the sustainable development of the SADC region.

C.   DEEPLY CONCERNED THAT:

i)   While some SADC member states have made some progress towards gender equality and gender mainstreaming, disparities between women and men still exist in the areas of legal rights, power-sharing and decision-making, access to and control over productive resources, education and health among others;

ii)   Women constitute the majority of the poor;

iii)   Efforts to integrate gender considerations in SADC sectoral programmes and projects have not sufficiently mainstreamed gender in a co-ordinated and comprehensive manner.

D.   RECOGNISING THAT:

i)   The SADC Council of Ministers in 1990 mandated the SADC Secretariat to explore the best ways to incorporate gender issues in the SADC Programme of Work, and approved in 1996 gender issues at the regional level to be co-ordinated by the Secretariat;

ii)   In execution of this mandate, the SADC Secretariat has developed and maintained working relations with key stakeholders in the area of gender, which resulted in the approval and adoption of the SADC Gender Programme by the SADC Council of Ministers in February 1997.

WE THEREFORE:

E.   REAFFIRM our commitment to the Nairobi Forward Looking Strategies, the Africa Platform of Action and the Beijing Declaration and Platform for Action.

F.   ENDORSE the decision of Council on:

i)   The establishment of a policy framework for mainstreaming gender in all SADC activities, and in strengthening the efforts by member countries to achieve gender equality;

ii)   Putting into place an institutional framework for advancing gender equality consistent with that established for other areas of co-operation, but which ensures that gender is routinely taken into account in all sectors;

iii)   The establishment of a Standing Committee of Ministers responsible for Gender Affairs in the region;

iv)   The adoption of the existing Advisory Committee consisting of one representative from Government and one member from the Non-Governmental Organisations in each member state whose task is to advise the Standing Committee of Ministers and other Sectoral Committees of Ministers on gender issues;

v)   The establishment of Gender Focal points whose task would be to ensure that gender is taken into account in all sectoral initiatives, and is placed on the agenda of all ministerial meetings;

vi)   The establishment of a Gender Unit in the SADC Secretariat consisting of at least two officers at a senior level.

G.   RESOLVE THAT:

As leaders, we should spearhead the implementation of these undertakings and ensure the eradication of all gender inequalities in the region;

AND

H.   COMMIT ourselves and our respective countries to, inter alia,

i)   Placing gender firmly on the agenda of the SADC Programme of Action and Community Building Initiative;

ii)   Ensuring the equal representation of women and men in the decision-making of member states and SADC structures at all levels, and the achievement of at least 30 percent target of women in political and decision-making structures by year 2005;

iii)   Promoting women's full access to, and control over productive resources such as land, livestock, credit, modern technology, formal employment, and a good quality of life in order to reduce the level of poverty among women;

iv)   Repealing and reforming all laws, amending constitutions and changing social practices which still subject women to discrimination, and enacting empowering gender-sensitive laws;

v)   Enhancing access to quality education by women and men, and removing gender stereotyping in the curriculum, career choices and professions;

vi)   Making quality reproductive and other health services more accessible to women and men;

vii)   Protecting and promoting the human rights of women and children;

viii)   Recognising, protecting and promoting the reproductive and sexual rights of women and the girl child;

ix)   Taking urgent measures to prevent and deal with the increasing levels of violence against women and children;

x)   Encouraging the mass media to disseminate information and materials in respect of the human rights of women and children.

IN WITNESS WHEREOF, We, the Heads of State or Government of the Southern African Development Community, HAVE SIGNED THIS DECLARATION.

DONE at Blantyre on this 8th day of September 1997, in two original texts, in the English and Portuguese languages, both texts being equally authentic.

Republic of Angola
Republic of Botswana
Kingdom of Lesotho
Republic of Malawi
Republic of Mauritius
Republic of Mozambique
Republic of Namibia
Republic of South Africa
Kingdom of Swaziland
United Republic of Tanzania
Republic of Zambia
Republic of Zimbabwe

LIST OF NATIONAL PARTNERS AND CONTACTS IN 12 SADC COUNTRIES

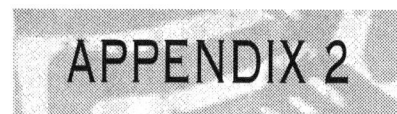

APPENDIX 2

ANGOLA
REDE MULHER
Emilia Fernandes, Secretary General
Avenida Hoji ya Henda
No. 21 1° Andar, C.P. 16532
Luanda, Angola
Tel/ Fax: 244-2-449513
E-mail: rede.mulher@netangola.com
sgmulher@netangola.com

BOTSWANA
WOMEN'S NGO COALITION
Vivian Gunda, Director
Extension 12, Machechele Road
Plot 3316
Gaborone, Botswana
Tel: 267-3185004/5
Fax: 267-3184685
E-mail: womens_ngo_coa@info.bw

LESOTHO
WOMEN AND LAW IN SOUTHERN AFRICA
(LESOTHO)
Keiso Matashane, National Coordinator
The Dolphin House
23 Motsoene Road, Industrial Area
Maseru, Lesotho
Tel: 266-22-313123
Fax: 266-22-310361
E-mail: wlsales@ilesotho.com

MALAWI
WOMEN AND LAW IN SOUTHERN AFRICA
(MALAWI)
Seode White, National Coordinator
Off Grevellia Avenue
Private Bag 534
Limbe, Malawi
Tel: 265-1-641534
Fax: 265-1-641538
E-mail: wlsamalawi@sdnp.org.mw
wlsamalawi@hotmail.com

MAURITIUS
MAURITIUS ALLIANCE OF WOMEN
Kokila Devi Deepchand, President
Royal Road
Quatre Bornes, Mauritius
Tel/Fax: 230-4243489/4252362
E-mail: m.a.women@intnet.mu

MOZAMBIQUE
FORUM MULHER
Maria da Graca Samo, Executive Director
Rua Pereira do Lago
N147, 3 Andar Direito, C.P. 3632
Maputo Mozambique
Tel/Fax: 258-1-493437/490 255
E-mail: forum@forumulher.org.mz
gracasamo@forumulher.org.mz

NAMIBIA
UNIVERSITY OF NAMIBIA
Social Sciences Division
Eunice Iipinge, Coordinator, Gender Training
and Research Programme
340 Mandume Ndemufayo Avenue
Pioneers Park, P. Bag 13301
Windhoek, Namibia
Tel: 264-61-2063954/3051
Fax: 264-61-2063268/3050
E-mail: eiipinge@unam.na

SOUTH AFRICA
UNIVERSITY OF WESTERN CAPE
Gender Equity Unit
Mary Hames, Director
Bellville 7535, Modderdam Road
P. Bag X17
Cape Town, South Africa
Tel: 27-21-9592813
Fax: 27-21-9591314
E-mail: gender@uwc.ac.za
mhames@uwc.ac.za

SWAZILAND
WOMEN AND LAW IN SOUTHERN AFRICA
(SWAZILAND)
Lomcebo Dlamini, Acting National Coordinator
P.O Box 508 Mbabane H100
First Floor, Portuguese Club, Commercial Road
Mbabane, Swaziland
Tel: 268-404-1732/7088/1723
Fax: 268-404-6750
E-mal: wlsaszd@africaonline.co.sz

TANZANIA
TANZANIA GENDER NETWORKING
PROGRAMME (TGNP)
Mary Rusimbi, Executive Director
Mabibo Road
P.O Box 8921
Dar Es Salaam, Tanzania
Tel: 255-22-2443205/2443450/2443286
Fax: 255-22-2443244
E-mail: info@tgnp.org
mary.rusimbi@tgnp.org

ZAMBIA
ZAMBIA ASSOCIATION FOR RESEARCH AND
DEVELOPMENT
Beatrice Simwapenga-Hamusonde
Executive Director
16 Manchichi Road, Northmead
P.O Box 37836
Lusaka, Zambia
Tel: 260-1-224536
Fax: 260-1-222883
E-mail: zard@microlink.zm

ZIMBABWE
ZIMBABWE WOMEN RESOURCE CENTRE
AND NETWORK
Caroline Chikoore, Executive Director
288 Hebert Chitepo Avenue
P.O Box 2198
Harare, Zimbabwe
Tel: 263-4-758185
Fax: 263-4-720331
E-Mail zwrcn@zwrcn.org.zw

APPENDIX 3

Names of People Who Provided Information for Various Sections of the Draft and Validated the Manuscript

Name	Job title/organisation	Address
Susan Nkomo	Chief Executive Officer The Presidency-Office on the Status of Women	P.O Box 268, Pretoria 0008, South Africa Email: susan@po,gov.za
Nomboniso Gasa	Researcher/ Political and Gender Analyst/ Freelance Writer	119 Eckstein Street Observatory P.O Box 2224, Bedfordview 2008, South Africa E-mail: chisana@wol.co.za
Mary Hames	Director Gender Equity Unit, University of the Western Cape	Gender Equity Unit, University of the Western Cape, Private Bag X17, Bellville, 7535, South Africa Email gender@uwc.ac.za
Professor Cathi Albertyn	Director Centre for Applied Legal Studies University of the Witwatersrand Gender Research Programme	University of the Witwatersrand Centre for Applied Legal Studies Private Bag 3, Wits University 2050, South Africa Email albertync@law.wits.ac.za
Dr Cheryl Hendricks	Political Researcher / Lecturer	46 Rouwkoop Road Rondebosch, 7700, South Africa
Dr Desiree Lewis	Independent Researcher/Writer and Lecturer	34 Roberts Road, Woodstock, 7925, South Africa
Ms Penny Paranzee	Currently researcher on the Women's Budget at IDASA,	6 Spin St, Cape Town, 8001, South Africa
Dr Yvette Abrahams	Researcher/Writer Manager of the Herstory Project	University of the Western Cape, Private Bag X17, Bellville. 7535, South Africa
Professor Amanda Gouws	Lecturer/Researcher/Writer Political Science Department, University of Stellenbosch	Political Science Department, University of Stellenbosch, Private Bag X1, Matieland, 7602, South Africa
Ms Glenise Levendal	Manager	Local Government Programme Gender Advocacy Programme, Ruskin House, Roeland Street, Gardens, 8001, South Africa
Ms Nontle Beja	Office Manager	Gender Equity Unit, University of the Western Cape, South Africa
Ms Vanessa Ludwig	Programme Officer	Gender Equity Unit, University of the Western Cape, South Africa
Ms Karin Koen	Independent Consultant	170A Caroline Street, Brixton, 2092, Johannesburg, South Africa
Ms Patricia Handley	Lecturer/Independent Researcher	51 Cape Bay, Athol Avenue, Somerset West, 7130, South Africa